What Does
the Bible
Say About... **?**

Life and Death

"What Does the Bible Say About...?" Series
Ronald D. Witherup, P.S.S.
Series Editor

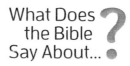

What Does
the Bible
Say About... **?**

Life and Death

John Gillman

New City Press
Hyde Park, New York

Published by New City Press
202 Comforter Blvd.,
Hyde Park, NY 12538
www.newcitypress.com

Cover design and layout by Miguel Tejerina

Biblical citations are taken from the New Revised Standard Version
©1989 Division of Christian Education of the National Council of the
Churches of Christ in the United States of America.
Library of Congress Cataloging-in-Publication Data

What does the Bible say about Life and Death
Library of Congress Cataloging-in-Publication Data: 2020931322

ISBN 978-1-56548-405-4 (paperback)
ISBN 978-1-56548-406-1 (e-book)
ISBN 978-1-56548-697-3 (series ISBN)

Printed in the United States of America

Contents

Series Preface

The Bible remains the world's number one best-seller of all time. Millions of copies in more than two thousand languages and dialects are sold every year, yet how many are opened and read on a regular basis? Despite the impression the Bible's popularity might give, its riches are not easy to mine. Its message is not self-evident and is sometimes hard to relate to our daily lives.

This series addresses the need for a reliable guide to reading the Bible profitably. Each volume is designed to unlock the Bible's mysteries for the interested reader who asks, "What does the Bible say about...?" Each book addresses a timely theme in contemporary culture, based upon questions people are asking today, and explaining how the Bible can speak to these questions as reflected in both Old and New Testaments.

Ideal for individual or group study, each volume consists of short, concise chapters on a biblical theme in non-technical language, and in a style accessible to all. The expert authors have been chosen for their knowledge of the Bible. While taking into account current scholarship, they know how to explain the Bible's teaching in simple language. They are also able to relate the biblical message to the challenges of today's Church and society while avoiding a simplistic use of the biblical text for trying to "prove" a point or defend a position, which is called "prooftexting"—an improper use of the Bible. The focus in these books is on a religious perspective, explaining what the Bible says, or does not say, about each theme. Short discussion questions invite sharing and reflection.

So, take up your Bible with confidence, and with your guide explore "what the Bible says about LIFE AND DEATH."

Introduction

The stories of life and death in the Bible invite us to delve more deeply into our own story and those we hear from others—like this one. The call came for a chaplain to visit Maria, a new mom, and Sarah, her infant daughter, in the maternity unit of a large medical center in Southern California. The Pacific Ocean was in view from the top floor of the hospital. Usually, such referrals are to provide a blessing for the newborn and to share in the joy of the mother and the gathered family. This case was different.

Less than a mile away, in the ICU of another hospital, there was a young man, the victim of a drive-by shooting. Barely clinging to life, he had no hope for recovery. He had been declared brain dead, and the ventilator was about to be removed and all aggressive care stopped. His mother was Maria. I was that chaplain, faced with the impossible task of supporting Maria as she rejoiced in the birth of her newborn while overcome with unspeakable waves of grief at the senseless death of her son.

In one bewildering day the mystery of life and death collided in the heart of one mother. All I could do, with the help of God, was to be present with her and her cauldron of emotions. The anger and rage, the profound grief, the comfort of holding onto Sarah ever more closely. I often wondered how she managed to cope once she left the hospital. As Maria's future unfolded, how would she tell the story? How would her fractured heart find healing? What resources would she draw upon? Would she find anything in her Christian tradition, or the Bible, to show her the way and bring her comfort?

From the opening chapters of Genesis in the Old Testament to the final segment of Revelation, the last book in the New Testament, the themes of life and death course through the biblical narrative like two intermingled streams in a river of humanity, indeed of all creation. Sometimes the waters rage as they did for Maria in her joy and her grief. The torrents can seem overwhelming. I think of blameless Job and his unmerited suffering. His wife urged him to curse God and die (Job 2:9). In other passages the currents overflow with joy and gladness as they did for Elizabeth, whose child leapt in her womb, and for the pregnant Mary, whose spirit rejoiced in God her Savior (Luke 1:44-48).

Now to the dawn of my own story. It was a snowy Christmas day on the third floor of a small community hospital. My mother had been in labor for several hours and it was not going well. My father was worried. In later years my parents related, though without going into great detail, that my mother almost didn't make it, and I was at risk of never seeing the light of day. On this day when the new life of a helpless infant born in Bethlehem was being celebrated around the world, my own life in tranquil Batesville, Indiana, was nearly doomed to darkness. Through the grace of God, I made a healthy appearance as dusk settled in, and thanks be to the Creator, my mother lived until she was nearly ninety-one. The mystery of life and death apparent once more.

In these short chapters we'll touch on several complex questions that confront us about being alive, staying alive, and dying. Throughout, whether you see yourself as a believer or non-believer, religious or non-religious, spiritual or secular, or simply are unsure, I invite you to join the conversation. Perhaps there are aspects of your own story that remain unexplored, questions you have tucked away for some later date, or experiences of death and loss that remain in the shadows of your inner being. As you journey through this brief narrative, I invite you to explore your experiences and to engage others in theirs around the issues of life and death.

Chapter One

The Dawn of Life

You are here. I am here. And according to recent estimates there are 7.7 billion others who take up residence on planet earth. From a sheer biological perspective, it is amazing that you and I as unique individuals have been given the breath of life, rather than never having come into existence. That a "me" or a "you" comes into being is nothing less than incredible.

We can push the story back a bit. That our parents even met—mine at a community dance hall in the small hamlet of St. Mary's, Indiana—is its own mystery. Whether the pregnancy was planned or unplanned, whether we were wanted or unwanted, the forces of nature pushed us into the life that is now ours. From a biblical perspective, the activity of the Divine was paramount. The prophet Jeremiah, even though he faced a surfeit of suffering, received this word from the Lord: "Before I formed you in the womb I knew you" (Jeremiah 1:5). The reminder that we have been known by God since before our beginning may offer tremendous comfort.

When things turn out well in life, we tend to rejoice, thinking that God is smiling upon us. On the other hand, if we have been dealt a lousy hand, we may feel warranted in wrangling with the deity as Jeremiah did later in life, when he cursed the day he was born (Jeremiah 20:14), or as the psalmist complained who felt banished "in the regions dark and deep" (Psalm 88:6). Yet even in those moments of desperation both prophet and psalmist continued to trust in a God who encouraged them and remained their strength (Jeremiah 33:1-26; Psalm 18:1-2).

The question of how it all began is addressed through two remarkably different Creation narratives by two different writers at the beginning of Genesis. According to biblical specialists, their accounts were probably influenced to some extent by other similar creation stories from the Ancient Near East, such as the Gilgamesh Epic, an Akkadian poem. Before taking a closer look at the Genesis narratives, it is helpful to recall that the writers' intent in these chapters was not to give a literal or scientific report of the dawn of the universe, the origin of species, or in particular the appearance of the first humans. Instead, their purpose was broader and more theological. Their aim was to explain through story and poetry the creative power behind creation. This was none other than the one God, the Lord (YHWH, the four-letter designation for the God of Israel, whose name was not to be pronounced).

The Creation of the Heavens and the Earth

The first Creation account (Genesis 1:1—2:3) is launched with these momentous words: "In the beginning when God created the heavens and the earth . . ." (1:1). Out of a formless void and darkness God's creative power brought into being the domains of light, the land and the waters, the blooming vegetation, and all forms of living creatures who fill the waters, the sky, and the earth (1:1-25). That this happened in seven days connotes completeness. Echoing throughout the narrative we hear this positive divine appraisal seven times: "God saw that it was good," with the emphatic "very good" at the end, accentuating the value of humankind in the eye of the divine.

This salutary reminder urges all of us to join our voices with the psalmist who breaks out in praise for God whose majestic glory fills the heavens and the earth (Psalms 8 and 148). The Jesuit poet Gerard Manley Hopkins captures this well in his eloquent exclamation, "The world is charged with the grandeur of God."

When did the universe begin? Scientists generally agree that its origin stretches back about 13.8 billion years, that our solar system made its appearance about 4.5 billion years in the past, and that life first appeared some 3.8 billion years ago. Approaching creation with a sense of wonder, the writers of Genesis address the theological question of how planet earth and all that it contains, along with the heavenly lights, came to be. As the one who brought into being all that is, both animate and inanimate, God, the sovereign power, is acclaimed. The *Catechism of the Catholic Church* affirms that "creation is the beginning and the foundation of all God's works" (198), that God needed "no pre-existing thing or any help in order to create," and that God "creates freely 'out of nothing'" (296).

The Creation of Humans in God's Image

As the pinnacle of creation, God "created humankind in his image [Hebrew ṣelem], / in the image of God he created them; / male and female he created them" (Genesis 1:27). The Hebrew term that is usually rendered as "image" has also been translated as "likeness," meaning representation. Elsewhere, the term is used to describe a statue.

This verse probably inspired Michelangelo's iconic portrayal of the creation of Adam—one of the majestic panels depicting scenes from Genesis—among the frescoes on the ceiling of the Sistine Chapel. The last time I visited there I spent several minutes, as have so many, straining upward to take in this masterpiece of grace and movement. The right hand of God, portrayed as an older, bearded, yet muscular man floating on a nebulous form, stretches out toward, though does not quite touch, Adam. Mirroring God's gesture, Adam extends his left hand toward this powerful figure. The divine index finger almost, but not quite, connects with the human. The implication is that, when contact occurs, life will be given to Adam and all humankind.

Naming humans as images of God indicates that they are not God but rather resemble God, in the sense that they have a divine mandate to rule over all creation. In a similar vein, the psalmist is ecstatic in praise of God who made human beings "a little lower than God, / and crowned them with glory and honor," and who has "given them dominion over the works of your hands" (Psalm 8:5, 6). On the other hand, Psalm 104 portrays humankind as part of the created order, not its master. The universal claim that everyone manifests God's image cautions us whenever we tend to look upon another person as less than others.

Because God brought humans, both male and female, into being, they have great dignity. Their life is sacred, for it is a gift of God and precious to behold. In the Gospels Jesus quotes Genesis 1:27 in a dialogue with the Pharisees to underscore the profound union of male and female creating one flesh (Mark 10:6). St. Paul adds a profoundly Christological dimension to this verse from Genesis when he proclaims that Christ is the image of God (2 Corinthians 3:18, 4:4) and that believers are destined to bear the image of Christ (1 Corinthians 15:49).

All human persons, regardless of cultural background, socio-economic status, or sexual orientation, profoundly reflect who God is, and as such are God's representatives. They share in divine life itself. The Church Father Irenaeus (d. ca. 202 AD) articulates well the intimate connection between the divine and the human: "For the glory of God is a living man [man fully alive]; and the life of man consists in beholding God."[1] (Of course, today we would use "human" or "humankind" to be clear that it includes women.) To become fully human is nothing less than profound participation in the divine!

To deeply connect with another human person, where heart speaks to heart, where embodied spirits engage, and where mutual respect flourishes is to experience a glimpse of the Holy One. For each person uniquely and tangibly reflects the very being of the Creator who blessed all humankind. God commanded male and female to participate actively in the creative life-giving process itself: "Be fruitful and multiply" (Genesis 1:28).

The Church teaches that "every spiritual soul is created immediately by God" (*CCC*, 366). Precisely when humans first appeared on the face of the earth involves the disciplines of science. It is generally accepted by anthropologists that *Homo erectus* ("upright man") emerged on the scene about 2.8 million years ago (based on fossils discovered in Ethiopia), and that *Homo sapiens* ("modern" humans) arrived about 300,000 years ago. As mentioned above, the writers of Genesis are not so much interested in *when* humans appeared but rather in the Creator God who overcame chaos, darkness, and emptiness in order to bring about life and the conditions to sustain life.

The process of creation is dynamic and ever unfolding through successive epochs. New species arise and die out. Tectonic plates shift, continents adjust. Heavenly bodies burn out and new stars appear. Volcanic activity gives rise to new islands emerging in the oceans. As the mythic story unfolds, human generations are chronicled. Calling to mind such movements on a cosmic scale, St. Paul personifies all creation as a mother in labor when he describes the longing for redemption: "We know that the whole creation has been groaning in labour pains until now" (Romans 8:22). And God's people too are groaning as they await God's new world yet to be born.

This new world is disclosed to the visionary in the Book of Revelation, who "saw a new heaven and a new earth," indeed the "new Jerusalem" (Revelation 21:1, 2). In this totally transfigured metropolis, life will be radically transformed, for "death will be no more"; nor will there be mourning, crying, or pain (21:4). The original creation in Genesis and the new creation in Revelation are jubilant bookends to the often-fractious relationship between God and humankind, a relationship restored by Christ, "the image of the invisible God, the firstborn of all creation" (Colossians 1:15). For in Christ is the fullness of all things, both in heaven and on earth (Ephesians 1:10).

God's Life-Breath Imparted to the Human

We turn now to the second Creation account (Genesis 2:4-25). The tradition from which this writing developed probably predates the first by about four hundred years. This narrative offers a more earthly rendition of human origins. Depicting God as a craftsman, the writer explains, "God formed man from the dust of the ground" (2:7). Then, with a marvelous, human-like gesture, connecting divine body with human form, God "breathed into his nostrils the breath of life [*nishmat hayyim*]; and the man became a living being [*nephesh hayah*]" (2:7). The breath of God not only brings life but also marks the divine origin of the person. Human life begins with this God-given breath and ends when breath departs.

That humans are created from dust in Genesis chapter 2 is a harbinger of the human body's ultimate destiny, poignantly communicated in the Ash Wednesday ritual.

The highly popular practice of receiving ashes on the first day of Lent evokes for the participants the transient nature of the natural body and the call to repentance. The ashes are the remains of burnt palm branches that were carried ceremoniously in a solemn processional entrance on Palm Sunday of the previous year. The minister uses these to make the sign of the cross on the foreheads of the recipients, saying either "Remember that you are dust, and to dust to you shall return" (see Genesis 2:7; Jonah 3:6), or "Repent and believe in the Gospel" (see Mark 1:15). As a sign of repentance, the Ninevites in the Book of Jonah were instructed to cover themselves with sackcloth and sit in ashes (3:5-6).

The term *nephesh* in Genesis 2:7, meaning "soul" or "life force," is the animating principle of the human. Following the creation of Adam, in a second step, God fashions from a rib of Adam (whose name literally means "a creature of the earth") a suitable helpmate, whom the first man calls Woman (2:21-23).

Throughout history some have used this account as support for the subordination of women. To buttress his argument that women were to have their heads veiled when they pray, St. Paul argues that "man was not made from woman, but woman from man" (1 Corinthians 11:8). Yet, seemingly as a corrective, he affirms that "just as woman came from man, so man comes through woman; but all things come from God" (verse 12). And then in his famous egalitarian proclamation, Paul declares, "there is no longer male and female; for all of you are one in Jesus Christ"

(Galatians 3:28). These last two verses would appear to tip the Pauline balance to the side of equality.

The first woman becomes for Adam "bone of my bones / and flesh of my flesh" (Genesis 2:23). The man and woman enjoy life together; though naked, they were not ashamed. On a broader level this account communicates an essential aspect of human nature. To be and to thrive as a person is fundamentally to be in relationship, and through relationship to flourish and grow into one's full potential. Anything that hinders, tarnishes, or prevents such relationships diminishes the grandeur of what God has wrought.

A very moving, maternal description of the divine creation of humans is found in Psalm 139: "For it was you who formed my inward parts; / you knit me together in my mother's womb," for which the psalmist acclaims: "I praise you, for I am fearfully and wonderfully made" (139:13-14). In the mysterious process of gestation God is already at work (see Jeremiah 1:5). This affirmation gives serious pause to threats experienced today from multiple directions to terminate the life of the unborn *in utero*, as we will discuss in chapter three.

Delight in Human Life

Humans are to delight in life. By following the "path of life" they will experience "fullness of joy" and "pleasures forevermore" in God's presence (Psalm 16:11). The "path of life" implies an ethical dimension and refers to the ways of God expressed by remaining faithful to the covenant and its obligations. In the book of life are written all the days of the faithful (Psalm 139:16), but one's enemies will be "blotted out of the book of the living" (Psalm 69:28). Harsh judgments like the latter are to be held alongside God's mercy.

The book of life metaphor implies that God is a record keeper of one's name and deeds on earth. Yet in this respect it is helpful to recall that God is not a cold-hearted auditor, but one filled with mercy and compassion, for God's "anger is but for a moment; / his favor is for a lifetime" (Psalm 30:5).

Similar to the Psalms, though without the emphasis on the covenant, Qoheleth's answer to good living is to delight in life while you have it. Nothing is better under the sun than for people "to be happy and enjoy themselves as long as they live" (Ecclesiastes 3:12). (Ecclesiastes is a Greek translation of the Hebrew Qoheleth.) As in Proverbs, young men are instructed to "enjoy life with the wife whom you love" (9:9). Qoheleth commands: "Go, eat your bread with enjoyment, and drink your wine with a merry heart; for God has long ago approved what you do" (9:7). Do that now, for after death this will be impossible.

Enjoyment is to be found in feasts, wine, and money for "Feasts are made for laughter; / wine gladdens life, / and money meets every need" (10:19). Those who delight in a fine glass of wine after a hard day at work know this well. The message of Ecclesiastes, informed by the culture and belief of its time, is to relish life now, for this is when we receive all God's blessings and rewards.

On a more profound, theological level, we turn to the Gospel of John, where Jesus succinctly announces his purpose: "I came that they may have life, and have it abundantly" (John 10:10). This promised bountifulness would consist, not in stone water jars filled to the brim with water turned into wine as at Cana, but in eternal life available in the present to all those who believe. From the dawn of life at Creation to the abundant life proclaimed by the Messiah, the biblical narrative reaches its climax. However, there is an underside to life, at least physical life, and so we now step into that realm, the reality of death.

For Reflection

- In what ways do you, through your person and your actions, reflect to others the image and likeness of God?

- How do you relish God's good creation and nourish a grateful heart for the life you have been given?

Chapter Two

The Shadow of Death

The results from pathology came back. The news was devastating. The shock hit her like a tsunami. LaVera, a successful attorney at a prestigious law firm in Los Angeles, was told by her oncologist that her stage IV breast cancer had metastasized to her bones, liver, and lungs. After six months of intensive treatment, she had lost weight, her hair, and her stamina. With a year at most to live, her dreams of seeing her daughter and two sons grow up, graduate, and marry had evaporated. One afternoon in the kitchen Katrina, her five-year-old daughter, asked, "Mommy, why do you have to leave us and die?" The torrent of tears did little to alleviate her overwhelming grief.

Why do we have to die? From earliest times humans have faced this inscrutable, agonizing question. The writers of Genesis address this conundrum with an event in the garden. After such a promising beginning when humans enjoyed the fullness of a carefree life with God, things quickly take an ominous turn. Sadly, in the Garden of Eden Adam and Eve squander the gift of life. Expelled from the bliss of paradise, their destiny is marked by the shadow of death.

There are two trees in the account: the tree of life and the tree of the knowledge of good and evil. The first provides for everlasting life and the second gives moral knowledge, but also brings death for those who partake of its fruit. In the first divine words to a human person in the Bible, God utters this command: "You may freely eat of every tree of the garden; but of the tree of the knowledge of good and evil you shall not eat, for in the day that you eat of it you shall die" (Genesis 2:16-17).

Then an ordinary, though crafty, serpent—the devil, according to later interpreters—gets into the act, and attempts to undermine God's trustworthiness, with the counter promise "You will not die" (3:4). The first couple disobeys God and eats the fruit of the tree. Then their eyes were opened, and they knew that they were naked (3:7), an awareness that echoes the sexual overtones of the story. God expels them from the garden, and they continue to survive. Either God does not carry through with the threat of death, or death is used metaphorically referring to exclusion from the garden and the immediate presence of God. Whatever the case, once expelled, they could not eat from either tree. Can you imagine Adam asking God for a second chance, as Abraham boldly interceded with God to spare Sodom (Genesis 18:16-33)? Or making an emotional appeal: "God, do you really want to do this? Won't you be lonely walking in the garden by yourself?"

The Genesis account does not assume that humankind was immortal before the Fall. Instead, it tells how immortality, life forever with God, was almost gained but seemingly lost. Later, God reinforces human mortality, declaring: "My spirit shall not abide in mortals forever, for they are flesh" (Genesis 6:3). Just before this, in what has been called the "death chapter," we read that nine out of ten generations end with "and he died" (e.g. 5:5, 8, 11). However, the break with the divine is not definitive. After the garden encounter God does not separate from humanity entirely, for Enoch and Noah "walked with God" (5:22, 24, 6:9).

The penalty meted out by God for disobedience affects both the woman and the man. The former will bear children in pain, and the latter will earn bread by the sweat of his brow. God tells the man that he is made of the same material stuff as the earth: "you are dust, / and to dust you shall return" (3:19). These words echo down through the ages, such as when the minister marks foreheads with ashes on Ash Wednesday. Carrying this sign throughout the day vividly recalls our mortality. Similarly, with more families receiving the ashes of their deceased loved ones due to the increased practice of cremation today, they are graphically reminded of our eventual return to dust.

Letters to Death, our Destiny

Notice that in Genesis chapter 3 there is no mention of rebellion, guilt, or sin (whether original or otherwise). Rather this passage is more about human desire and fear. A firm connection between sin and death only comes later and is evident in the writings of St. Paul, pre-eminently in the Adam-Christ typology to be discussed below. As the account concludes, the man names his wife a second time, calling her Eve (*havāh*), which means "the mother of all living (*hay*)" (3:20). Ironically, although she ate the fruit that brought death, she became the mother of all succeeding generations. These represent for her a form of "eternal life."

So, why are we doomed to die? Genesis gives two different responses, one anthropological and the other moral. The first is simply that is how we were created: having been fashioned from the earth we are inherently mortal (2:7). The second is that the inevitable fate of death, the "return to the ground" (3:19), is a consequence of disobedience.

Since death is our destiny, is death the nadir of human life, and as such, our foe? Or, on the other hand, is it possible to recalibrate death as our greatest gift, as Henri Nouwen does in one of his last books?[2] Toward the end of a course on death, dying, and afterlife, which I've been offering for college students, I ask them to address a letter to death, responding to the question: "Do you see death as a friend or a foe?" Surprisingly, most of them choose the former.

One student began his letter, "Dear Death, I hope you've been well [!], I just wanted to thank you for not letting me be immortal. I am a believer that your presence makes things more meaningful. You are the ultimate reason to not procrastinate on [getting] things [done]. You are the deadline I don't want to miss." Another begins audaciously, "Dear Death, You do not scare me; I am not frightened by you. ... I believe that death is something that reminds us of the importance of our lives, and to find purpose in it."

Still another felt bedeviled by death from an early age: "Dear Death, I knew you for a long time. ... At a young age, I hated you so much and you terrified me as well. Now, after understanding you more, I am less hating and fearing you. ... You always made me sad and depressed when you took away some of the people I love."

In pastoral care, I have often spent time with residents in nursing homes who long for death to deliver them from their pervasive experiences of boredom and pain, both physical and emotional. On the other hand, those in the prime of life who, like LaVera, have received a terminal diagnosis, see death as the enemy, to be fought with every ounce of strength they can muster. Whether death is appraised as friend or foe—many will experience both, even within a short time span—each of us without exception, as the poet John Donne famously put it, is eventually the one "for whom the bell tolls." Not knowing the time, the place, or the circumstances of the foreboding knell, humans cannot escape that moment when the bell "tolls for thee."

The psalmists remind us that death is the inevitable end of life on earth (89:48); it is the destroyer of bonds between the living and the dead, exerting its power in the land of the living. It lurks behind the corner for the severely ill person who cries out: "O LORD, heal me, for my bones are shaking with terror" (6:2); it is like a "deadly thing [that] has fastened on me" (41:8). In dire straits, the petitioner cries out: "The cords of death encompassed me; / the torrents of perdition assailed me; / the cords of Sheol entangled me; / the snares of death confronted me" (18:4-5). The "cords"

28

may refer to the nets and nooses that Death and Sheol, like hunters, have set for the afflicted person, or they may point to the cloth bands used to bind up the corpse.

Not unrelated is the situation of those who today linger in intensive care units, connected to a web of tubes and beeping machines whose aim is usually to keep death at bay. Complex ethical questions often arise. What are the patient's preferences about the use of aggressive medical treatment on the one hand, or comfort care on the other hand? When do the latest technological interventions and pharmacological resources serve to bring healing and return the afflicted to an acceptable quality of life, and when do they interfere with the dying process? Sharing the psalms quoted above may provide spiritual support to those who come face to face with death, and who may feel conflicted between the determination to keep fighting and the desire to let go.

Goodness and Kindness in the Shadow of Death

One of the most well-known psalms that provides comfort and reassurance in the face of death is Psalm 23. This is a beloved spiritual resource that many from all faiths throughout the world draw upon during troubled times, particularly when death approaches. It is used at memorial services to bring solace to the bereaved. Portraying the Lord as the divine shepherd, an Ancient Near Eastern metaphor for royalty, the psalmist experiences restoration of the soul (verse 3), guidance through the valley of the shadow of death (verse 4) and refreshment at God's own table (verse 5). Verse 4a is sometimes translated as "a valley of deepest darkness," a metaphor for severe distress and the nearness of death. To look into the darkness can be very healing, as it was for Elaine Pagels and Julie Yip-Williams, authors of recent memoirs on death and dying.[3] The experience of the psalmist's deliverance may have given rise to this song of trust.

The shadow of death came upon our family when a younger athletic sister—she was only fifty-seven—died of acute leukemia after a valiant struggle. The shadow of death had its grip on a colleague, a Gold Star mother, whose twenty-one-year-old son's life was cut short when his vehicle hit an IED in Iraq. The shadow of death surrounds all those who suffer the loss of a loved one. Some seem to remain in this shadow, even despairing of life itself, unable to work through the throes of grief. Others, sustained by their faith and supported by a caring community, find a way through the dark clouds and rediscover the joys of life little by little.

While most would not concur with the psalmist of Psalm 23 that all the days of our lives are marked by "goodness and mercy," there is hope. The imagery is rich: peaceful waters that bring restoration; a rod and staff that provide comfort; the divine host at a banquet table that celebrates joy; anointing that offers strength; and an overflowing cup that represents abundance. Happiness consists in dwelling "in the house of the LORD / my whole life long" (verse 6). This last line is often understood as a reference to the next life.

With candor Psalm 23 and several others acknowledge the reality of death that accompanies human life. This takes us back to Genesis chapter 3, but also forward to the Apostle Paul, who reshapes the story of Adam in Genesis by drawing a close connection between sin and death (Romans 5:12-21; 1 Corinthians 15:20-22, 55-56), a link not made in the original account of the fall. Paul explains that through Adam sin came into the world, that through sin death entered, and that death spread all across the planet. Sin becomes the inevitable environment which all of us perpetuate through our own misdeeds (Romans 5:12-14). As earthly creatures made of dust we all participate in the humanity and the mortality of Adam (1 Corinthians 15:22, 47-48).

Besides sin and death, law also gets into the act, for law is the power of sin (1 Corinthians 15:56). What the law forbids entices a person to sin (Romans 7:7-12). It is helpful to recall that Paul offers different perspectives on the law. On the positive side the Apostle affirms that the law is holy and good. Nonetheless, death, sin, and the law form a troublesome trifecta. For Paul this trio affects all of us. It is especially the power of sin and death that threatens to overtake our life with Christ.

The Last Adam, the Life-giving Spirit

Now for the good news! According to Paul, in God's plan there is another Adam, and this is Christ, the one with life-giving power. Far surpassing, overriding, and nullifying the negative impact of the first Adam's transgression (which brought death), the last Adam offers the gift of God's grace made abundantly available for all who would receive it (Romans 5:15-16). This divine benefit restores the right relationship between God and humanity. By creatively adapting Genesis 2:7, Paul contrasts the first Adam who became a living being with the last Adam who became a life-giving spirit (1 Corinthians 15:45).

Paul professes his convictions about the life-giving spirit, having personally been surrounded by the shadow of death on multiple occasions. Without going into detail, he soberly shares with the Corinthians the affliction he experienced in Asia, when he and Timothy "were so utterly, unbearably crushed that we despaired of life itself." He adds, "Indeed, we felt that we had received the sentence of death" (2 Corinthians 1:8-9). Perhaps he is referring to the terrible ordeal he experienced while imprisoned in Philippi (Philippians 1:19-24) or to that elusive event when he fought "with wild animals at Ephesus" (1 Corinthians 15:32). The latter reference is probably not to a literal encounter with killer beasts, but rather a metaphorical allusion to the hostile powers he faced in preaching the gospel.

Jesus too was shadowed by death, almost from the beginning of his public life. Early in the Gospel of Mark the evangelist notes that the Pharisees conspired with the Herodians on "how to destroy him" (Mark 3:6). Immediately after the narrative reaches its turning point with Peter's profession that Jesus is indeed the Messiah (8:29), Jesus reiterates three times that the Son of Man must undergo great suffering resulting in death (8:31-32, 9:30-32, 10:33-34).

As his fate drew near, Jesus went to Gethsemane with Peter, James, and John, where he "began to be distressed and agitated" (Mark 14:33). Baring his soul to these select three apostles, Jesus revealed the staggering state of his agony and vulnerability: "I am deeply grieved, even to death," asking them to remain with him and stay awake (14:34). They remained; they did not stay awake. The writer of Hebrews amplifies Jesus' distress, saying that he "offered up prayers and supplications, with loud cries and tears" to God, the one "who was able to save him from death" (5:7).

Jesus had made a direct and unapologetic appeal to "Abba, Father," pleading that the Father "remove this cup" from him. Then almost in the same breath, letting go of any need to be in control, he relinquished his ultimate destiny into the hands of God: "not what I want, but what you want" (Mark 14:36). Still, while on the cross he utters a seemingly implacable plea: "My God, my God, why have you forsaken me?" (Mark 15:34; a quotation from Psalm 22:1). The evangelist portrays Jesus as on the precipice of despair, nearly overcome by the jaws of impending death encroaching upon him. But as many have suggested, with this outcry Jesus has not lost his trust in God, for the second part of the psalm he quotes expresses the hope that God will come quickly to his aid and ultimately deliver his soul (Psalm 22:19-20).

Death is real; it casts its shadow upon all humanity. In spite of all human efforts to avoid being swallowed by its grasp, it comes. Though for many decades there have been concerted, often ingenious efforts to ignore or shove aside this inconvenient reality, its sting remains. Ernest Becker's Pulitzer Prize-winning *The Denial of Death*[4] documents the valiant efforts that humans have made to circumvent this event by, for example, devoting themselves to "immortality" projects that transcend death. Nonetheless, the shadow of death has not evaporated. The ongoing challenge for each of us is to embrace our mortality, and from a faith perspective, to do this in a way that leads, not to despair, but to the hope and conviction that death and the shadow it casts do not have the last word. The living God through the risen Christ does not abandon us in the transition to the mysterious darkness of death but instead leads us through to a life on the other side.

For Reflection:

- Do you see death as primarily friend or foe, a blessing or a curse, a reality to be feared or to be embraced?

- Which deaths of loved ones have affected you most and how has your faith served as a resource in coming to terms with them?

Chapter Three

Darkness at the Origin of Life

At two months old the nearly-blind child was not supposed to return alive to the home of her cunning grandmother. But she did. She was also hardly expected to escape from war-torn Vietnam in 1975. But she did. And the odds were stacked heavily against her and her family when they made their harrowing escape across the South China Sea to Hong Kong in a dreadfully overcrowded tiny boat. But they survived. These events anchor the narrative that Julie Yip-Williams recounts in her captivating memoir, *The Unwinding of the Miracle*, mentioned in the previous chapter.

When the grandmother noticed that the odd milky whiteness in the eyes of her newborn granddaughter was robbing her of sight, she acted decisively. She determined that no one would ever love this blind girl, much less want to marry her. So the grandmother ordered the docile parents to take their daughter to an herbalist and request that he give her medicine to end her suffering. A man of character, the herbalist firmly replied, "I don't believe in this sort of thing. I'm sorry."

Exceeding the wildest expectations, Julie made it to America, graduated from Princeton, and earned a law degree from Harvard before landing a position with a prestigious firm in New York. Having miraculously survived the infanticide plot, she married a handsome Southerner and became the mother of two talented daughters. After starting her fragile existence largely clouded in darkness, Julie went on to live a courageous, productive, and happy life, only to have it implode with a diagnosis of stage IV colon cancer resulting in her death at forty-two.

Infanticide is the killing of a child within a year of birth. As attempted with Julie, infanticide is illegal in most countries, though it is still practiced and remains a scar on our contemporary landscape. Sex selection is one of several motivating factors.

The few instances in the Bible of this form of killing send chills down one's spine. The tenth plague brought about the slaughter of every firstborn among Egyptians, a punishment that dealt the final blow to a defiant Pharaoh (Exodus 11:1—12:32). A drastic act intended to free an oppressed people, it demonstrates not so much God's anger as it does God's sovereignty in the narrative of the Book of Exodus. With respect to child sacrifice, the Torah absolutely forbids this abhorrent act practiced by some groups to appease their gods (Leviticus 18:21, 20:3; Deuteronomy 12:30-31, 18:10) and to which the Israelites themselves succumbed more than once (Jeremiah 32:35; Ezekiel 16:20).

Fast forward to the infancy narrative in Matthew's Gospel. Infuriated when he heard about the child who had been born king of the Jews, Herod ordered "all the children in and around Bethlehem who were two years old or under" to be killed (Matthew 2:16). The Church celebrates the Feast of the Holy Innocents on December 28, recalling in the liturgy that they "were crowned with heavenly grace" on account of the Savior's birth. Endearingly, Jesus lays his hands on "little children" (*ta paidia*), showing them special care "for it is to such as these that the kingdom of heaven belongs" (Matthew 19:14). He upholds them as examples of true humility, dramatically subverting the disciples' focus on rank and importance (Matthew 18:1-5).

A separate but related situation is that of abortion, the intentional termination of an unborn fetus, whether done chemically by a pill, by a procedure in a clinic, or in some other fashion. Abortion has raised complex ethical and legal issues, both past and present, not only for the mother and the baby, and sometimes the father, but also for society at large. The Hippocratic Oath as taken by some physicians (originating ca. 400 BC) states: "I will not give a woman a pessary [medication-soaked wool] to cause an abortion."[5] In the landmark case of *Roe v. Wade* (1973), the Supreme Court argued that the unborn fetus is not a person as understood in the Fourteenth Amendment to the U.S. Constitution and ruled that abortion is a fundamental right. In no way has this resolved the issue in a divided country where the debate continues to rage. Both sides have appealed to the Word of God to bolster their argument.

Even in My Mother's Womb

The Bible does not directly address abortion. Those texts that are discussed relative to this topic need to be carefully and cautiously considered. There are several texts which imply that life comes from the first breath (for example, Genesis 2:7; Ezekiel 37:10), yet can one infer from these passages that their intent is to exclude the possibility of life in the womb, and therefore that the Bible does not forbid abortion, as some proponents claim? The Bible does not scientifically pronounce when life begins or philosophically decree whether a fetus is a person. In fact, Scripture contains no word for fetus, although it does speak figuratively about "the fruit of the womb" (Isaiah 13:18; Psalm 127:3; also Luke 1:42). Nonetheless, a number of biblical texts figure prominently in the abortion debate, with both sides advancing conflicting interpretations in the battle to gain moral ground. (The monikers "pro-choice" and "pro-life" are thickly layered with multiple emotional, legal, and ethical dimensions; they will be used here cautiously.)

Since humans are commanded to subdue the earth and have dominion over it (Genesis 1:28), some conclude that responsible stewardship includes mastery over the fate of the unborn. Not so fast, others argue, since the narrative's larger context places clear limits on human freedom (Genesis 2:8-9,15-17; see 1:29-30). Human life belongs to God, but does this in itself make it sacred? Because God's supreme act of creation confers on humankind the unique dignity of being fashioned in the image of God (1:27), for some it is a small step to conclude that human life is itself sacred, for such is God's name. Whoever sheds human blood will pay the ultimate price, "for in [God's] own image / God made humankind" (9:6). While Genesis does not address the status of the fetus in the womb, several biblical passages suggest that God is active in the unborn.

In prophetic speech, Jeremiah records his call from God: "before you were born I consecrated you" (Jeremiah 1:5); similarly Isaiah announces, "The LORD called me before I was born" (Isaiah 49:1). Echoing language from the prophets, Paul believes that even before his birth God called him and by divine grace set him apart (Galatians 1:15). The psalmist poetically extols the marvelous process of gestation: "For it was you who formed my inward parts; / you knit me together in my mother's womb" (Psalm 139:13). The diligent agency and providential care of the Creator was already in play before birth, even before conception. Since this is God's work, the life of the unborn is to be respected. But some pro-choice voices dismiss these texts because their genre is poetic rather than scientific. Furthermore, they argue that these texts speak about exceptional individuals, namely inspired prophets and a psalmist.

However, such a view unfortunately discounts the larger symbolic world of the Bible, which conveys profound spiritual truths about God's knowledge, and indeed, fashioning of the unborn. Would the Creator privilege the status of prophets and psalmists in a singular way that excludes all others created in the divine image? Such selectivity would be hard to defend, especially in the case of the psalmists, who write not exclusively for themselves but have in mind the elevated status of all humankind. Psalm 139:13 seems to specify the global affirmation of Psalm 8:5—that God has made human beings "a little lower than God, / and crowned them with glory and honor"—with particular attention to the creative role of the Divine in the unborn, as we saw above.

Nonetheless, retrospectively, some wish that they never saw the light of day. Albeit impertinently, Job in anguish queries God: "Why did you bring me forth from the womb? / Would that I had died before any eye had seen me" (Job 10:18). Though deeply distraught, his spirit broken, Job musters the courage to challenge God for his undeserved suffering (13:20—14:22), until finally God speaks, not answering Job's questions directly but expounding on the wonders of cosmic realities. Job finds a modicum of peace with God, for "now my eye sees you" (42:5).

As I reflect on Job's distress, I recall a difficult pastoral care dialogue where the issue of a regretted birth also surfaced (Job in his lament cursed the day he was born, wishing that "that day be darkness" [Job 3:4]). Joel, a sixteen-year-old diagnosed with a schizoaffective disorder, felt bullied by peers and unloved by both his mother and God. He blamed himself for his parents' divorce, later disclosing to his shocked mother what he overheard in a late night spat between them—that his dad wished that his mom had had an abortion "because I was nothing but trouble." The pain of being unwanted continued to fester deep within; Joel's search to make sense out of his troubled life was ongoing. Through compassionate intervention by the social worker and the chaplain, Joel seemed to take a step toward finding some meaning for his existence, and thus drew closer to the spirit of Job's response to the Lord at the end of the book: "I know that you can do all things, / and that no purpose of yours can be hindered" (42:2).

Let's return to the biblical witness and look at the life of Rebekah. While pregnant with twins, she is deeply troubled when she feels them struggle in her womb: "If it has to be this way, why do I live?" (Genesis 25:22). The note of despair she strikes is not unfamiliar to pregnant women and fathers today faced with dire circumstances. In this instance, the outcome is mainly positive. Rebekah lives and Esau and Jacob are born. Their sibling rivalry continues, yet God uses their contentious relationship—and Jacob in particular—to carry out the divine promise to make of Abraham (their ancestor) a great nation.

Turning to the Book of Exodus, we come across a hypothetical legal case where trouble is brewing (21:22-25). A fight breaks out between two men in the presence of a pregnant woman. If the expectant mother is injured during the fracas, causing a miscarriage (the word used in the NRSV) but no further harm, the judges should rule that the responsible combatant is to pay whatever the woman's husband demands. However, if other harm follows, the penalty shall be "life for life, eye for eye . . ." Halakhic (Jewish law based on the Torah) exegesis reasons that since the punishment is monetary in the first scenario and capital in the second, the unborn is not considered a person.[6] Some pro-choice advocates underscore this inference. (Note that the Hebrew for Exodus 21:22 reads "and her children come out," in other words, are born prematurely, thus creating a very different scenario.)

However, the ambiguity in the text precludes a decisive interpretation. The narrative does not indicate whether the "children" come out alive. If so, no harm was done. If not, then the penalty of "life for life" would seem to come into play, and thus make the passage an argument against intentional abortion. Yet this rendering may read into the brief scenario more than what is apparent. Since intentional abortion is not mentioned in this passage, its relevance for the debate has been questioned.

The Challenge of New Testament Passages

Much attention in this conversation is given to Luke 1:44. When Mary greets her cousin Elizabeth, who is pregnant with John the Baptist, Elizabeth feels movement in her womb. When she heard Mary's greeting, her relative says, "the child [Greek, *brēphos*] in my womb leaped for joy." The literal meaning for *brēphos* is "unborn child, embryo." Months before, an angel had announced to Zechariah that "even before his birth" their son "will be filled with the Holy Spirit" (Luke 1:15). These texts render human dignity to the pre-natal child to be named John. Is this an exceptional case? Not in the view of Clement of Alexandria, who, on the basis of these Lukan texts, argues that a fetus is a human person with a soul.[7]

The majestic prologue in the Fourth Gospel gives singular prominence to God as the author of life: "All things came into being through him, and without him not one thing came into being. What has come into being in him was life, and the life was the light of all people" (John 1:3-4). Celebrating God as the source of life, the evangelist implies that life neither originates with nor belongs to us. This conviction undergirds the presumption held by many Christians against any effort to legitimate the termination of human life, whether at its origins, its full development, or its waning years.

The Position of the Church and the Christian's Responsibility

The earliest undisputed reference to the prohibition of abortion and infanticide is found in the *Didache*, also known as *The Teaching of the Twelve Apostles*, which dates to the late first or the early part of the second century. The anonymous writer inveighed against abortion: "You shall not murder a child [*teknon*] by abortion nor kill them when born" (2.2), a text also translated "you shall not abort a child or commit infanticide." This became the position of the Church in succeeding ages down to present times and is encoded in the *Catechism of the Catholic Church* (2270-2275). Beginning with conception, every human person is decreed to have the inalienable right to life. Thus, Pope John Paul II, canonized a saint in 2014, stated in his encyclical *The Gospel of Life* (1995), "I declare that direct abortion, that is, abortion willed as an end or as a means, always constitutes a grave moral disorder, since it is the deliberate killing of an innocent human being" (62).

While the official position of Catholicism on the right to life is patent, there is a pressing need on the pastoral level to address the agonizing choice that women with a medically complicated or an unwanted pregnancy face. Significant numbers of the women facing unwanted pregnancy are from minority groups who are impoverished and feel disenfranchised. Put in positions where they have scant authority over their bodies and circumstances, they are often dominated and abused by men. The picture is especially bleak for those in dire economic situations as well as for those in war-torn countries forced to flee for their lives, and in the process are threatened, kidnapped, and raped. When pregnancy results, they are forced to make excruciating decisions about the fate of the unborn child who came to be through the violence and intimidation of an overpowering, despised impregnator.

In response to these and the plenitude of untold stories, three biblical passages present themselves.[8] One is the Good Samaritan (Luke 10:25-37). Jesus turns the question posed by the clever lawyer about neighbor classification on its head: "Which of these ... was a neighbor to the man who fell into the hands of the robbers?" (10:36). How has the Christian community become neighbor to those, some of whom are victims, carrying an unwanted child? Where is the support, the compassion, the heartfelt love? A second text, Luke's portrayal of the close-knit group of believers in Acts, suggests that their generosity was such that there was "not a needy person among them" (Acts 4:32-35).[9] How is the Christian community to respond today to the needs of those with unwanted pregnancies? "The vulnerable" for whom we are to care encompasses the pregnant woman, the child in the womb, and perhaps the father, who may or may not be around to shoulder his responsibility. In addition, the wellbeing and the spiritual health of the community is also affected.

And this brings us to Paul the Apostle, who has sometimes garnered mixed reviews regarding his stance on women (compare Galatians 3:28 and 1 Corinthians 14:34-36). Paul's eloquence about the unity of the body of believers who make up the Body of Christ (1 Corinthians 12:12-26) leaves one uneasy when a blind eye is turned to any single member. Paul writes: "If one member suffers, all suffer together with it; if one member is honored, all rejoice together with it" (1 Corinthians 12:26). There are many exemplary cases when the Christian community has stepped forward to help pregnant women and families who may feel ill-equipped to bring the unborn to full term or who are anxious about how to provide financially and emotionally for a newborn.

Occasionally difficult ethical dilemmas are faced today when the lives of both the mother and unborn child are in mortal danger. In a well-publicized case some years ago, Joyce, a twenty-seven-year-old mother of four children who was eleven weeks pregnant, after seeking consultation, had an abortion of her non-viable unborn child at a Catholic hospital. Without this medical intervention, both mother and child would have died. Several ethicists, both Catholic and non-Catholic, supported the mother's heart-rending decision. The local bishop, however, disagreed. He censured the Catholic hospital and stripped it of its Catholic identity. Would further dialogue marked by deep listening, guided by respect for all lives involved—mother, father, and child—and by the fullness of biblical witness, have led to a different outcome?

Throughout the centuries, the Church has clearly enunciated its position in defense of the sacredness of life for the unborn. The assembly of God's people—the root meaning of the church, the Greek word *ekklēsia*—has a less stellar record in stepping up to "bear one another's burdens," thus fulfilling "the law of Christ" (Galatians 6:2). The task before us is to increase our awareness and respond compassionately to those who may be suffering silently, facing a seemingly impossible dilemma.

For Reflection:

- Within your own community, how might there be a greater safety net and a welcome outreach for an expectant mother facing an unwanted pregnancy and for all those involved to come forward and seek support?

- Choose a biblical text about new life from this chapter to read, ponder, and pray over using, perhaps, the method of *lectio divina* (Latin for "Divine Reading"), a traditional practice of reading Scripture reflectively, meditation, and prayer.

Chapter Four

The Path of Life

In chapter one we explored the dawn of life, in chapter two, the reality of death, then in chapter three considered infanticide, new life in the womb, and the complex topic of abortion. We turn now to explore in broad strokes the biblical paradigm of life from birth to death. How is this to be lived out? What characterizes a life well lived? Where do we turn to find guides, and what are the signposts along the way that keep us headed in the right direction in our quest to live an abundant life?

For believers the ultimate guide to true life is the living God about whom the psalmist proclaims: "You show me the path of life. / In your presence there is fullness of joy" (Psalm 16:11). Even in the face of present danger or at the end of earthly life (16:10), the petitioner trusts that the Lord God will enlighten the faithful with the path of life. The final destination brings the fullness of unending joy—a gift of the Holy Spirit (Galatians 5:22)—in the divine presence. Since life was in God and that life served as the light for all people, as the Fourth Gospel proclaims (John 1:4), the person of faith readily looks to God for guidance along the path to be traveled, and looks pre-eminently to the Word-made-flesh who himself is the Way (John 14:6).

Peter, in his address on Pentecost, applies Psalm 16 to the risen Christ who becomes the path of life (Acts 2:25-28). The challenge, of course, is to discern divine guidance in Jesus the Messiah and to harmonize one's will with the mind of Christ.

From creation there is implanted in each human person a thirst for the living God (Psalm 63:1), or as Ronald Rolheiser calls it, a holy longing.[10] This pining for the Divine is manifested in one's restless heart and aching desire. Burning in each of us, with varying degrees of intensity, is a fire that longs for the most that life can offer, and so we search, pushing the envelope at times, even to the edge of a precipice.

When the enticing highs of unbridled power, the accumulation of wealth, and unrestrained sexual expression reign supreme, all may seem well and good, at least momentarily. But the perceived benefits accorded by these paths of life are really not that at all. Instead they lead inevitably—whether acknowledged to oneself or not—to isolation, discontent, and disillusionment. However, when the influx of the grace of Christ and the Spirit is warmly received, some make a course correction and realign their values. Having weathered the crucible of painful experience, lost relationships, and self-serving behaviors run amok, they search anew for the path of life, this time guided by a wholesome spirituality grounded in a relationship with the Creator. A new or re-discovered path of life is also signaled by concern for the overlapping values of the common good, social justice, and the wellbeing of the community.

When I ask college students about their dreams, their hearts' desires, or their career choices, many respond that they want to make a difference in this world, to find happiness, and to share life with someone they love. Some already know what career path they want to pursue, for example, that of a pediatrician, an environmentalist, or an occupational therapist. Others struggle to find clarity and seem lost without direction. Still they search. Sometimes their path comes serendipitously. Recently while getting a hearing exam from an audiologist who was as skilled as she was passionate about her profession, I asked what led her in this direction. Her response surprised me. She had always wanted to be a teacher, but there were no openings in the class she needed, so she ended up in a class on audiology. She found her path. Over the course of twenty years she has assisted many to hear more clearly.

The Path to Life

The path to life often involves circuitous twists and turns. For several years I have known Travis, now in his mid-sixties. When he was young and idealistic, he joined the Peace Corps, where he met his wife when both of them served in Thailand. Then he returned to his home state and spent the next twenty-five years working in a hardware store. Though mildly successful, he felt an underlying discontent. He wanted to connect in more meaningful ways with those who are facing struggles. After he completed his M.A. in Theology, he went on to become a hospice chaplain, specializing in the art of being present with patients experiencing dementia. He discovered that bringing butterflies to his patients, sometimes placing one on their finger, was a way to invite their trapped spirit to emerge, whether in a simple smile or an open gesture. In that sacred encounter a glimmer of light became manifest, at least for a moment .

The Gospel of Luke is on one level a story of searchers. In their encounter with the Baptist, the herald of the Messiah, three groups of inquiring bystanders—the crowds, the tax collectors, and the soldiers—ask this lone voice in the wilderness the fateful question: "What should we do?" (Luke 3:10-14). John calls all of them to change course and act courageously: give to the needy, conduct yourselves honestly, and don't abuse your authority.

Later in Luke's account both a lawyer and a ruler press Jesus with a question about securing life in the next realm: "What must I do to inherit eternal life?" (10:25-37; 18:18-26). To the lawyer Jesus tells the story of the Good Samaritan, concluding with a surprising twist by redefining the meaning of neighbor. The question Jesus puts before him is not "who is your neighbor?" but instead, how are you a neighbor to those like the person beaten and left half dead on the roadside? In other words, your path of life is to become neighbor yourself, helping any human being in need whom you are in the position to assist. A few chapters later, to the seemingly content law-abiding ruler who was also seeking eternal life—or simply asserting his moral credentials to the "Good Teacher"—Jesus raises the bar: "Sell all that you own and distribute the money to the poor, and you will have treasure in heaven" (18:22). Those contented with their current path of life, however praiseworthy, may be called to make uncomfortable, even radical, choices.

Among those who have made life-altering decisions to follow the path of the one who "set his face to go to Jerusalem" (Luke 9:51) are many among the communion of saints, including St. Francis of Assisi, Dorothy Day (social activist and advocate for the poor), Blessed Stanley Rother (American diocesan priest martyred in Guatemala) and St. Elizabeth Ann Seton (wife, mother of five children, founder of a religious community). Their paths to discipleship were not the routes of least resistance. In his youth an avid socialite who relished wild parties, Francis later defied his father, a wealthy cloth merchant, left behind a luxurious life, and chose a path marked by humility, simplicity, and dedication to repairing God's house. Dorothy Day started houses of hospitality, offering food, clothing, and community for those needing shelter. She lived among the poor she served on the lower east side of New York City. She renounced war as an instrument of policy. She knew that the answer to the long loneliness she felt was to be found in community. Through arrests, threats, and conflicts, her faith sustained her along life's path.

Stanley Rother said yes to the promptings of grace and left behind the comfort and security of life in Oklahoma to serve the poor in Santiago Atitlán, Guatemala. He learned the Tz'utujil language and started a radio station to transmit daily lessons. And then he was murdered. Having been warned earlier that his life was in danger, he replied: "This is one of the reasons I have for staying in the face of physical harm. The shepherd cannot run at the first sign of danger." Elizabeth Ann Seton lived through many difficulties, including the death of her husband, and believed that her own troubles would teach her how to comfort others. She founded a religious order to care for the children of the poor, the Sisters of Charity of St. Joseph; she was determined to serve the Lord with every breath she drew.

From the Narrow Gate to the Cloud of Witnesses

"Enter through the narrow gate," the master taught; "for the gate is wide and the road is easy that leads to destruction, and there are many who take it. For the gate is narrow and the road is hard that leads to life, and there are few who find it" (Matthew 7:13-14). The emphasis in this hard saying is not that only a select few will be saved but rather on the demands of discipleship on the road that leads to life. This is often the road less taken, running counter to that followed by the great majority. As the Gospel account unfolds, we encounter the gentle side of Christ, who conveys this message to ordinary people: "Come to me, all you that are weary and are carrying heavy burdens, and I will give you rest" (Matthew 11:28). Resting in the gentle and humble heart of Jesus the Messiah along life's journey lightens one's burdens and offers respite.

Jesus himself experienced this need for rest. When he and the disciples had no respite even to eat because so many were going and coming into their lives, he called them to "come away to a deserted place all by yourselves and rest a while" (Mark 6:31). There is a renewed emphasis today on the need to care for body, mind, and spirit by setting aside Sabbath time. In removing ourselves from the tedium of text messaging, the blare of ever-running news cycles, and the buzz of daily chaos marked by schedules, deadlines, and routine tasks, we allow ourselves to renew our spirit and get needed perspective on our way of being. To set aside such quiet times in a peaceful place allows us to refresh ourselves, and thus to be better equipped to observe the commandment, "You shall love your neighbor as yourself," central to both Old and New Testaments (Leviticus 19:18; Mark 12:31).

For almost everyone the school of love begins in the family, for that is where most of us are launched and nourished along the path of life. Whether the family unit is understood traditionally, or more broadly as it is today, referring to all those who live under one roof, the family ideally includes nurturers—parent(s) and others—as well as those being nurtured. Many are the people in the home whose ordinary lives are unremarkable yet whose faithfulness in their life journey has a profound impact on those entrusted to their care.

Though largely uncelebrated and little noticed except by those dear to them, these too are among the great "cloud of witnesses" (Hebrews 12:1), women and men, from Sarah and Abraham up to the present day. Each of you will know who these unsung heroes are in your life. I myself am mindful of a young woman who grew up on a farm during the Depression. For the first three years of her education, she walked to a one-room brick schoolhouse on a county road. She met the love of her life on a dance floor of a small country town in southern Indiana. Georgene dedicated herself to the wellbeing of her ten children. A gifted seamstress, she made dresses and quilts for children and grandchildren. Her life was a tapestry of love. When her husband was on the verge of death, having suffered a broken back from a traumatic fall, she never gave up hope for his recovery. Her faith sustained her in difficult times. Throughout her ninety-one years, she gave herself fully to the wellbeing of others. She was my mother.

Choices in the Family

For many the path of life is manifested in raising, forming, and guiding children, whether one's own or those who make up the larger family of relatives and friends. Most often children are experienced as a source of blessing to their parents. As described poetically in the psalms, they are like olive shoots / branches around one's table (Psalm 128:3-4). When the family gathers for a festive thanksgiving meal, parents and grandparents often beam with joy as they see their offspring interact, even with the teasing and tensions, the sibling squabbles, and the little ones squirming. God's first commandment in the Bible, "be fruitful and multiply" (Genesis 1:28), is being fulfilled. For the larger community of faith, the younger generation represents promise and hope. Stories are shared, traditions are handed down, and life prospers.

From one generation to the next, people on the path of life go forward, shaped by those before them, discovering in the process the unique person they were created to be. Wherever their journey takes them, whatever their life circumstances, they will undoubtedly experience, in the words of Moses, "life and prosperity, death and adversity" (Deuteronomy 30:15). Through it all, the ups and downs, the successes and disappointments, they are to "choose life," by loving and staying in relationship with the Creator, for that will lead to a life that is genuine and authentic (verses 16-20).

In many families, however, choices are made and behaviors displayed that run counter to the wellbeing of self and others. Relationships are fractured, grudges are nourished, and the paths to authentic life are compromised. The most extended account of family relationship in Genesis is that of Joseph, his brothers, and their father Jacob. The narrative centers on Joseph, the favored, beloved son of his father. Sold as a slave, then established as a powerful ruler in Egypt, Joseph becomes the arbiter of life and death when his father and brothers suffer from severe famine. In exchange for bringing him their youngest brother Benjamin, he promises his brothers: "you will live ... you shall not die" (42:18, 20). Their path to life depended on the beneficence of the brother they once hated and conspired to kill. In the end Jacob gathered his family for his final blessing and instructed his sons to ask their brother

Joseph to forgive their wrong in harming him. In response Joseph wept and spoke kindly toward them. Harmony is restored, until a later generation when a new Egyptian king nearly obliterates the people, and they are saved only by the path to safety that God provides through the Sea of Reeds.

The most compelling story of a divided family Jesus recounts is that of a father and his two sons who took errant paths in the search for life's fulfillment and happiness (Luke 15:11-32). In this parable of the prodigal son, the younger son left home in the pursuit of success and the good life. He found neither. The elder son lived an obedient and dutiful life yet was caught in resentment and trapped by envy.

In one of the darker moments of his life when he struggled with depression, rejection, and loneliness, the world-renowned spiritual writer Henri Nouwen visited the Hermitage in St. Petersburg, where he was profoundly struck by Rembrandt's *The Return of the Prodigal Son*. Pondering this painting, Nouwen reflected on how he identified with the prodigal (younger) son every time he sought unconditional love "where it cannot be found." Similar to the elder son, Nouwen became aware of "the cold anger that has rooted itself in the deepest corners of my being." The liberating moment came when he realized that God's outstretched arms as father and mother (as depicted in the painting) were inviting him to let himself be found, to be known, and to be loved by the Holy One. Through this divine embrace he felt that, as the beloved of his heavenly Father, "I can walk in the valley of darkness: no evil would

I fear." The path to a joyful life free of resentment opened up for Nouwen as he listened to the voice calling him the Beloved.[11]

The colorful tapestry unfolding throughout the Bible in narratives, precepts, and poems displays for us a wealth of wisdom as we pursue our path of life. The Word of God is there for our instruction. The great cloud of witnesses, both in Scripture and beyond, also stands before us as inspiration and guidance. Not only that, we whose bodies are the temples of the Holy Spirit are called to be among their number, making manifest in our earthly pilgrimage the rich texture of God's creation by the way we live our lives.

For Reflection:

- As you reflect on your path of life, its twists and turns, what moments stand out when you have felt the guiding hand of God or that quiet inner voice leading you to authenticity and wholeness?

- Who in your life have served as role models and mentors, guiding you along the course of your life?

Chapter Five

Life Ended by the Human Creature

The view from the crest of the Coronado Bridge is spectacular. Sunlight glistens on the San Diego Bay, the wind charting the course for a ballet of sails. To the northeast is the skyline of America's finest city—a promotional moniker for San Diego—and further in the distance the majestic mountains keep watch. To the west are the waters of the Pacific and to the south the neighboring islands of Mexico.

On a bright clear day Gary, a twenty-nine-year-old sailor, stopped his car in the center of the bridge. He was distraught. His girlfriend had recently died in the emergency room from a drug overdose. Despondent and utterly alone, he decided to bring an end to his fractured life. He stepped up on the concrete barrier, the only obstacle between him and the placid waters below. Just as he was ready to jump, the wind unexpectedly changed direction and caught him off-balance, causing him to fall back onto the solid surface. He shared this story with me, feeling grateful for a second chance to get his life back on track. As I write about Gary's account now, I am mindful of the line from John's Gospel, "the wind blows where it chooses" (3:8). In the case of this now-thirty-five-year-old, it made the difference between life and death.

It is fairly well known that the incidence of suicide has been on the rise for the past several years, increasing by 33 percent between 1999 and 2017 (Center for Disease Control). In 2016 more than 45,000 people killed themselves in the U.S. Among men the rate is almost four times that for women. Taking one's life is now the tenth leading cause of death overall, and the second leading cause among college students. According to the Department of Veterans Affairs, an average of fifty veterans take their lives each day. The ravages of war continue to reach far beyond the battlefield.

Hans Küng, a well-known, prolific, and often controversial German theologian and Catholic priest, has written about assisted suicide as a possible option for his own exit from life. Diagnosed with Parkinson's and macular degeneration, a prelude to loss of sight, he confesses: "I don't want to continue to exist as a shadow of myself."[12] He states that "No person is obligated to suffer the unbearable as something sent from God," and adds "People can decide this for themselves and no priest, doctor or judge can stop them."

Behind the numbers and the notables are the individual stories closer to home. Few are those who would not have a personal acquaintance, a classmate, or a relative who took his/her own life. We'll return to the complexities of such jarring events after a brief look at suicide in the Bible. There are a few scattered references to this in the Old Testament, and just one brief mention in the New Testament.

Life Ended by One's Own Hand in the Bible

We'll take a brief look at each of the six cases of suicide in the Hebrew Bible, all men: Abimelech (son of Gideon), Samson, Saul, Saul's armor-bearer, Ahithophel, and Zimri. The unfortunate King Abimelech suffered a deadly injury when a woman dropped a millstone on his head and crushed his skull. In this dire state he was conscious enough to ask a young man to kill him with a sword, since he did not want it known that he was killed by a woman. His pride and fear of shame motivated the request. Strictly speaking, this would be called assisted suicide (Judges 9:53-54).

Samson brought about his own death in a dramatic fashion. Humiliated and blinded by the Philistines but strengthened by God, he brought down their temple as an act of revenge, thus killing many of the enemy and himself (Judges 16:25-31). His self-sacrifice borders on an act of martyrdom.

In a case similar to Abimelech, Saul commanded his armor-bearer to run his sword through him to escape being killed by the enemy, after he was badly wounded in a battle against the Philistines on Mount Gilboa. The man refused, so Saul "took his own sword and fell upon it." Then, seeing that Saul had died, the armor-bearer did likewise, out of devotion to his king (1 Samuel 31:3-5; 1 Chronicles 10:3-5).

Ahithophel, convinced that the victorious David would execute him as a traitor, decided to hang himself (2 Samuel 17:23). The final example is Zimri who, having committed treason (by assassinating the king) went into the royal palace, set it afire, and burned to death inside (1 Kings 16:18-19).

The reasons these biblical figures committed suicide ranged from seeking revenge or avoiding shame to ending suffering. Their manner of death was noted in a matter-of-fact way, largely without comment by the biblical writers.

The only instance of suicide in the New Testament is that of Judas. Matthew remarks that after Judas expressed remorse for handing over innocent blood (Jesus), he hanged himself (Matthew 27:4-5; see the different account in Acts 1:18), a form of death the ancient world considered shameful. (Since Judas' hanging in Matthew is probably influenced by the almost exact parallel with the death of the traitor Ahithophel [2 Samuel 17:23], its historicity is uncertain.) Perhaps as an expression of guilt and repentance, this apostle, whom Jesus called friend, ended his own life. There is no consensus among biblical scholars about Judas' motive in handing over Jesus. Receiving thirty pieces of silver may not have been the underlying rationale. In any case, Matthew does not pass judgment on him for taking his life, as later theologians do. Traditionally, interpreters have branded Judas a villain; some recent commentators have sought to rehabilitate him by portraying him as exercising a positive role in facilitating Jesus' death and thus advancing the overall drama of salvation. This latter effort is rather speculative.

Jesus and Paul, Their Lives in the Balance

The question of suicide is not completely absent in the life of Jesus. When Jesus predicted his death in John's Gospel, "the Jews" asked among themselves: "Is he going to kill himself? Is that what he means by saying, 'Where I am going, you cannot come'?" (John 8:22; compare 7:34 and 13:33). Jesus' willingness to lay down his life of his "own accord " (10:18), however, points to his desire to offer himself as a sacrifice for our salvation, not a desire to take his own life in a dramatic rhetorical move or to avoid suffering or shame.

Paul too seems to entertain the possibility of being able to choose—or does he wait for others to choose for him?—whether he will live or die. While in prison, he reveals his inner struggle to the Philippians: "For to me, living is Christ and dying is gain. If I am to live in the flesh, that means fruitful labour for me; and I do not know which I prefer [literally, "choose"]" (Philippians 1:21-22). Paul struggles internally, wrestling with the two options before him: to live—which is the "more necessary" for the Philippians—or to die and be with Christ, which is "far better" (verses 23-24). Paul's apparent desire to die reflects his awareness that to be joined with Christ eternally is his and our ultimate goal, and that his work of spreading the gospel may bring that about sooner rather than later, because of those who (violently) oppose Christ. But he also sees that it is God's will that he continue his mission as an apostle for a time.

As we have seen, the Bible notes a few examples of suicide in the Old Testament and one instance in the New Testament. These briefly mentioned acts are not discussed or evaluated. They are neither condoned nor condemned or even viewed negatively. It is not until St. Augustine of Hippo that we have a clear denunciation of suicide in the Christian tradition. It is seen then as a violation of the commandment, "You shall not murder." Similarly, Thomas Aquinas argues that since life is a divine gift, to take one's own life is to sin against God. In line with this tradition, the *Catechism of the Catholic Church* affirms: "Suicide contradicts the natural inclination of the human being to preserve and perpetuate his life" (2281).

In a change from decades past when those who died by suicide were not allowed a church burial, the *Catechism* recognizes that eternal salvation is not withheld from those who take their lives (2283). This sets the framework for a more pastoral approach that emphasizes God's boundless mercy and compassion, which far exceeds our own.

In recent years many experts, as Ron Rolheiser summarizes, note that suicide is most often "the result of a disease, a sickness, an illness, a tragic breakdown within the emotional immune system or simply a mortal bio-chemical illness."[13] This mitigates significantly the role of free choice in any such act. Rolheiser compares those who died by suicide to those who jumped to their deaths from the World Trade Center towers, because their lives were mortally threatened by burning fires and collapsing structures. Death by suicide can be seen as one way to escape the agony of unrelenting pain and the thick darkness of despair. Or to put it differently, it may be that those in despair were "seeking nothing but the meaning of their lives."[14] Although suicide may be more understandable or be viewed more leniently when committed by a person suffering from a mental illness, it is always a tragedy, particularly if the person felt so much mental or spiritual pain that they could imagine it ending no other way. Their death prevents the possibility of receiving help or improving, and leaves loved ones and acquaintances grieving.

A Glimpse at the Contemporary Scene

The initial reaction to suicide is often shock and disbelief. In 2016 Father Virgilio Elizondo, regarded as the founder of U.S. Latino theology and a leading scholar in liberation theology, took his life with a gunshot to his right temple while clutching a rosary in his left hand. He had been accused of sexual abuse with a minor. Feeling tired, fatigued, and empty, begging for mercy and forgiveness, he left a note with his final thoughts. He said, "[I] freely choose my moment" as a way of "giving my life to others." For him it was "not a suicide but a farewell gift."[15] His puzzling words seemed to have interpreted his death as a self-sacrifice to atone for his misdeeds. Not surprisingly, his death caused great pain among victims because they saw it as a way of avoiding punishment for his (unproven) crimes.

Suicide is not a crime in the U.S., although if a person is known to be a danger to self or others, he or she can be held securely for up to seventy-two hours or until it is decided that the individual is no longer at risk. In a growing number of states there are laws that provide for physician-assisted dying, also referred to by other related names. The term "suicide" is generally not used, probably because of its negative connotations. Beginning with Oregon, which passed the Death with Dignity Act in 1997, several states, including California, Colorado, the District of Columbia, Hawaii, Montana, Vermont, and Washington have such statutes. Several countries have legalized rather liberal policies regarding physician-assisted death. In Belgium the law applies to cases of "unbearable or untreatable suffering," in Switzerland to "old age," and in the Netherlands to newborns with disabilities.

Faith communities have been divided on this issue. Most oppose such legislation, including the Catholic Church, which has taken a lead role in the U.S. and elsewhere defending the right of individuals to have a natural death. Other churches support individual freedom in decision-making. These include the Methodists, the Unitarian Universalists, the Presbyterians, and the Society of Friends.

Because it has been at the vanguard of the opposition to physician-assisted death, the United States Conference of Catholic Bishops' position, as stated in the document "Ethical and Religious Directives for Catholic Health Care Services," will be briefly summarized here. Life is considered to be a precious gift from God. For this reason, "we are not the owners of our lives and, hence, do not have absolute power over life."[16] Therefore, "Catholic health care institutions may never condone or participate in euthanasia or assisted suicide in any way" (ERD 60). Additionally, the slippery slope factor is important to consider: assisted suicide legislation may lead to deaths that are not truly voluntary. It is also viewed as reflecting a bias against persons with disabilities, those with serious illnesses, and the elderly. Further, it undermines efforts toward pain relief.

On that slippery slope is the movement toward allowing euthanasia in broad terms. In some circles it is believed that the most compassionate response to those who are suffering is to alleviate them of their pain by sending them peacefully into oblivion. The term euthanasia means "happy death," but this is far from the case when people with a physical or mental disability, or who otherwise require "extra" care, are viewed as a blemish to some idealized society defined by the fittest and the brightest, the most creative and the most attractive. Euthanasia is illegal in most of the United States. As mentioned above, "aid in dying" legislation has made headway in some states, though not without court challenges.

The Teaching of the Church

In its public statements in response to physician-assisted death, the Catholic Church has pointed out several deficiencies in such legislation. These statements do not, however, use Scripture in support of its position, probably because the documents are intended for a broad audience in a secular society. When considering the biblical witness, here are some of the relevant themes. First, life should not be prematurely shortened because it is a gift from God, who is the author of all life. Second, determining that one's life is not worth living rejects the dignity of the human person, who has been created in the image of God (Genesis 1:27), for who she or he is, not for what she or he can do. Third, suffering, though not a good in itself, can have positive value; for example, it produces endurance and steadfastness (Romans 5:3; James 1:2-4). Fourth, ending one's life through a prescribed drug is a rejection of dependence on God. Fifth, such action is hard to justify in the face of the commandment, "You shall not murder" (Exodus 20:13; Deuteronomy 5:17).

While life is considered a precious treasure to protect and value, the duty to preserve life is not absolute. Ethically, patients may decide to forego medical procedures that do not provide a reasonable hope or benefit—thus enhancing the quality of life—or that impose an excessive burden. In instances when medical technology has no (or possibly very marginal) benefit for the individual, persons often make the wise and prudent decision to decline such interventions. When a ventilator-dependent patient is declared brain dead, determined in part by lack of blood flow to the brain, the rhythmic sounds of a respirator and the movement of the chest may give the false impression that the body is still alive. Unless a ventilator is being used to maintain the vitality of the organs for possible harvesting and donation, the compassionate response in this emotionally-trying scenario is to remove all external medical support so as not to interfere with the final stages of the dying process (see ERD 30 and 59).

Self-Sacrifice as an Act of Love

In the Gospel of John, Jesus teaches that the most compelling demonstration of love for another person is to give up one's own life for one's friends: "No one has greater love than this, to lay down one's life for one's friends" (John 15:13). The notion of dying for one's friends reflects what Aristotle said about friendship in his Nicomachean Ethics 9.1169a ("It is true of the good man … that he does many acts for the sake of his friends and his country, and if necessary dies for them"). Such sacrificial action is also a hallmark of the good shepherd who "lays down his life for the sheep" (John 10:11). Standing behind these statements in the Gospel is the cross.

The sacrifice of St. Maximilian Kolbe, a Polish priest and prisoner in Auschwitz, is an inspiring example. In reprisal for one escaped prisoner, the Nazis selected ten others to die, one of whom was Franciszek Gajowniczek, a man with a wife and children. Fr. Maximilian offered his life in place of this man. His request was granted, and he was killed on August 14, 1941. John 15:13 is also laden with meaning for those in the military. Soldiers, especially those on the frontlines of battle, sometimes courageously risk their own life and limb to save the lives of their fellow troops. Many of these men and women are Purple Heart recipients.

"Losing" one's life is at the heart of being a disciple. This is the great paradox that Jesus places before those who would follow him: "For those who want to save their life will lose it, and those who lose their life for my sake, and for the sake of the gospel, will save it" (Mark 8:35). To lose means to let go, to detach oneself from, to relinquish. Since Mark wrote to Christians being persecuted, probably in Rome, to lose one's life may have been meant literally, to be willing to die for their faith. In thus losing their earthly life, they are promised life that does not end, eternal life. This is the paradox of life through death.

To conclude: the consistent witness of Scripture is that human life is to be protected, honored, and respected. While there is no condemnation in connection with the few instances of suicide in the Bible, the over-arching theme is that God is the author of life. With that in mind, can one argue persuasively that God also intended humans to have a decision-making role in when life is to be terminated? Some within the faith community have taken this stance. Others have taken a strong position against this legislative and cultural development in the United States and world-wide, asserting that human life has inherent value no matter the circumstances.

For Reflection:

- From a faith perspective, what do you see as the arguments for and against suicide?

- What do you believe are the main reasons that a person may or may not opt for assisted suicide?

Chapter Six

Innocent Blood: From Death to Life

Today is Easter Sunday 2019. Today Christians around the world celebrate the resurrection of Christ. Today over 250 people were killed and hundreds more wounded by suicide bombs in a wave of terror in Sri Lanka. Most of the victims were Christians at church; they had just been praying for peace. Church roofs were blown off by insidious bombs; church benches were stained by the blood of the innocent. These martyrs testified not with their words but with their blood. Martyrdom is not an anachronism.

The Easter feast, the highlight of the Christian liturgical calendar, is all about the victory of Christ over sin and death. Yet on this day the carnage of death seems to have reigned supreme through evil acts by vicious terrorists working their nasty deeds. Just a week before, the historic Notre Dame Cathedral in Paris burst into flames—the fire apparently accidental—at a time when churches across Europe and Asia were under attack. In recent decades Christians have become one of the most persecuted religious groups. Many of them have been killed.

Martyrs are those persecuted and put to death because they refuse to renounce their faith. Some, like the Sri

Lankan Christians, became martyrs almost inadvertently, simply by the practice of their faith. The term martyr is from the Greek *martys*, which means "witness." Originally this word referred to those who testified, that is, bore witness to what they believed. It also took on a more specific meaning, designating those who gave witness through the shedding of blood, as did those whose lives were cut short in Sri Lanka. Throughout the Bible there are several accounts of people who gave their lives for what they believed.

One of the first examples from the Old Testament are the prophets of the Lord who were killed by Jezebel (1 Kings 18:4). A Phoenician princess, she became the wife of Ahab, a king of the northern kingdom of Israel. She incited her husband to abandon the worship of God and set up an altar to the Phoenician god Baal in Samaria. She died a violent death herself: her servants, by order of the future king Jehu, threw her out a window (2 Kings 9:31-33).

The Wise Will Shine Brightly

Centuries later, the apocalyptic Book of Daniel (probably written around 164 BC) recounts a story of martyrdom averted by divine intervention in 3:8-30 and the martyrdom of the wise in 11:29-35. The former narrative—whether historical or legendary is uncertain—is set in the sixth-century BC and involves three young men who are thrown into a fiery furnace by Nebuchadnezzar, a Babylonian king, because they refused to serve his god or worship the statue of gold (Daniel 3:12). Death by roasting in a fire was a relatively common form of capital punishment (see Jeremiah 29:21-23). Miraculously the three men, Shadrach, Meshach, and Abednego, were unharmed by the flames. To his surprise the king noticed a fourth figure in the furnace, portrayed as having "the appearance of a god" (Daniel 3:25). Early Christian writers, including Irenaeus and Tertullian, identified this heavenly agent who saved the three men with Christ.

The latter narrative refers to actions by the arrogant and tyrannical Antiochus IV Epiphanes, a Seleucid king (d. 164 BC). He raged against the holy covenant and desecrated the Jewish Temple by installing "the abomination that makes desolate" (Daniel 11:31), probably a statue of Zeus Olympus. In the face of this onslaught against their ancestral religion, those Jews loyal to God stood firm. These are called the wise, for they would give understanding to many. However, due to their loyalty to God, they were cut down "by sword and flame," whereby they were "refined, purified, and cleansed" (Daniel 11:33,35). Their non-violent witness serves as a profile in courage and example of resistance in the face of evil.

This raises the question of theodicy (the explanation of how a good God allows innocent suffering and evil), also addressed passionately by Job. What recompense is there for the righteous who suffer in this life? Will the faithful who die by the sword be relegated to oblivion? If so, would this not call into question the justice of God, whom the Israelites believed in and counted on for rewarding the good and punishing the wicked? If the virtuous are unrewarded and evildoers given a free pass, then the deity remains little more than a fickle and capricious figure who toys with the fate of humans with little regard for either virtue or vice.

God's fidelity through life and death is frequently lifted up in the Psalms. The psalmists firmly believe that God's "goodness and mercy shall follow me" (23:6), that God is "the stronghold of my life" (27:1), and that God "will ransom my soul from the power of Sheol" (49:15). The answer to the query, "Will you not revive us again, / so that your people may rejoice in you?" is a resounding "yes" (85:6). None other than God "redeems your life from the Pit, [and] crowns you with steadfast love and mercy" (103:4). For God has "ordained his blessing, / life forevermore" (133:3). Will the wise in Daniel, having met their death, ever taste "life forevermore"?

Yes, they will! The great prince, Michael, arose and his army was victorious. At that time the promise was made that "many of those who sleep in the dust of the earth shall awake." These are indeed the wise who "shall shine like the brightness of the sky." They will be "like the stars forever and ever" (Daniel 12:1-3). The death of the martyrs is vindicated through individual resurrection. This is the first time belief in the resurrection is articulated in the Old Testament. It would be taken over and developed by the Pharisees and the Christians, especially by St. Paul.

Noble Deaths, Noble Examples

The theme of martyrdom continues in Second Maccabees, written around the same time as Daniel. In one passage, a mother and her seven sons are arrested and ordered by Antiochus IV Epiphanes to eat pork, which would be a repudiation of their ancestral religion. Each son, one after the other, refuses and then is subjected to extreme torture and death. Throughout their ordeal the soon-to-be martyrs remain steadfast in their belief that "the King of the universe will raise us up to an everlasting renewal of life" (7:9).

Before the first son is put to death, mother and sons declare in unison: "The Lord God is watching over us" (7:6). Then in turn each son makes a profession of faith before his demise. For example, the third son, after offering his tongue and hands to be chopped off, professes his hope that he will get them back again, presumably at the resurrection, by now understood literally as a physical restoration of the body (7:11). Near death the fourth son pronounces that Antiochus, in contrast to his faithful band of brothers, will have no resurrection. The last son decries this inhumane torturer as an "unholy wretch, [the] most defiled of all mortals," and assures him that he will not escape God's judgment (7:34-35). (Antiochus later dies in misery [9:13-28] and his son is murdered.)

Last of all the mother herself dies, although the text does not give the details. Before her last son's death, she confesses, "I do not know how you [her sons] came into being in my womb. It was not I who gave you life and breath, nor I who set in order the elements within each of you," adding that the Creator of the world "will in his mercy give life and breath back to you again" (7:22-23).

Before their deaths, the sons pray that God will show mercy to their nation and that the wrath of the Almighty will come to an end through their deaths (7:37-38). Whether or not the brothers' deaths were vicarious, that is, undertaken on behalf of the people, they clearly served as an example to remain steadfast in times of persecution. The stories of their bravery in the face of death would have had a powerful impact. To a people fighting for their very survival, they would serve as an impressive example of tremendous courage and unfailing commitment.

Just prior to the narrative of the brothers in chapter 7, Eleazar, an old man, is also put to death. The author interprets his death as an example of nobility and a memorial of courage. For Eleazar wants to leave a noble example for the young of how to die a good death willingly and out of respect for revered and holy laws (6:28,31). And that he does.

In Second Maccabees, martyrdom becomes a type of divine worship. In response to intense suffering, God vindicates these righteous ones for their unwavering faith during times of extreme trial and torture by fulfilling their cherished hope for resurrection and eternal life. And indeed, after the martyrdom of Eleazar, the mother, and her sons, the tide begins to turn for the Jewish people, and they successfully fight off their oppressors. Not addressed, however, is why God allows those most faithful to experience extreme torture. (Keep in mind that the narratives in Second Maccabees are not to be read uncritically as historically accurate in every detail.)

The Witness of John the Baptist and Stephen

The first martyrdom we encounter in the New Testament is that of John the Baptist (Mark 6:17-29). This prophet condemned Herod Antipas for violating the Torah (Leviticus 18:16) because he married the wife of his brother Philip. Since the legality of a ruler's marriage in a religious state is not a private affair, John's attack could be perceived as sedition. Fulfilling a promise made to his wife's daughter, Herod gave her the head of John the Baptist on a platter, as requested by her vindictive mother. About John, Jesus said, "among those born of women no one has arisen greater than John the Baptist" (Matthew 11:11). He also castigates Jerusalem as "the city that kills the prophets" (Matthew 23:37), including John.

By speaking truth to power, the Baptist's dauntless stance ended in martyrdom. If John died before Jesus did, as the Gospels assume, we might ask how awareness of his cousin's martyrdom may have influenced Jesus' own courageous confrontation with his accusers during his trial and crucifixion. Jesus freely and willingly accepted his own death and thus became the preeminent model of martyrdom and the "faithful witness," as he is named in Revelation (1:5, 3:14).

Apart from Judas and John the beloved disciple, it is likely the other apostles died as martyrs. Acts reports that James, the brother of John, was put to death by a sword (Acts 12:2). According to the tradition, Peter and Paul, who became the two pillars of the Church, were martyred in Rome during the reign of Nero, although neither death is recounted in the New Testament. Ultimate allegiance is owed to God alone, not to any emperor. This Peter professes: "We must obey God rather than any human authority" (Acts 5:29). Also, the post-Easter Johannine community seems to have been aware that Peter, having stretched out his hands (on the cross), had endured martyrdom for the flock (John 21:18-19).

The first known martyr in the early Church is Stephen, a deacon "full of grace and power" (Acts 6:8), whose impassioned testimony about the works of God so enraged the Jewish council that they dragged him outside the city and stoned him to death (7:2-60). As intended by the writer, the parallels between Stephen's experience of dying and that of Jesus are striking. Stephen's vision of "the Son of Man standing at the right hand of God" (Acts 7:56; compare Luke 22:69), the relinquishing of his spirit (7:59; compare Luke 23:46), and the prayer of forgiveness for those complicit in his death (7:60; compare Luke 23:34) dramatize how Jesus serves as an efficacious model for future generations of Christians who are threatened with death.

Martyrs Past and Present

Writing during a period of Roman persecution, John of Patmos composed the Book of Revelation to encourage patient endurance and offer hope. He praises the martyrs, whose blood, shed for God, is "the blood of saints" (Revelation 16:6, 17:6). He singles out two witnesses, variously identified as the prophets Moses and Elijah or, from the more contemporary scene, the apostles Peter and Paul (11:1-14). After these witnesses finish their testimony, a beast—who in the author's symbolic universe represents Rome and its emperors—rises up from the pit. This sea creature conquers and kills the witnesses, and their bodies are left in the street of the city where "their Lord was crucified," one of the few references to the historical events of Jesus' life in Revelation (11:8). But then, after three days, the breath, the spirit, of God enters them and they arise. Then, summoned by a loud voice, they ascend to heaven (11:12).

In the first few centuries, until Constantine's Edict of Milan in 313 (which accorded Christianity legal status in the Roman Empire), martyrdom was viewed as the supreme witness to one's faith in Christ. Ignatius, bishop of Antioch (d. 107), who was arrested and sent to Rome, envisions himself as a cultic sacrifice with an intense longing to die in order to be with Christ. Writing to the churches, he expresses this plea: "Let me be fodder for wild beasts—that is how I can get to God. I am God's wheat and I am being ground by the teeth of wild beasts to make a pure loaf for Christ. I would rather that you fawn on the beasts so that they may be my tomb and no scrap of my body be left."[17]

We then come to the *Acts of Perpetua and Felicitas* (early third century). Arrested when she was taking classes for baptism, Perpetua (d. 203), a wife and mother, refused to offer sacrifice to the emperor, and thus was put to death. The source describes the active role she took to end her life: she, "being pierced between the ribs, cried out loudly, and she herself placed the wavering right hand of the youthful gladiator to her throat. Possibly such a woman could not have been slain unless she herself had willed it . . ." (6.4).[18] Both Ignatius and Perpetua seem to intensify the preference of Paul for whom "living is Christ and dying is gain" (Philippians 1:21). In a time and place when being Christian meant almost certain (public and violent) death, these witnesses had no wish to preserve their own lives at cost to their faith and their love for God.

In our own day we recall, for example, the tens of thousands of Vietnamese Catholics put to death (in the nineteenth century), the many Central American martyrs in recent decades, the seven French Trappist monks along with others murdered in Tibhirine, Algeria (1996), or the beheading of twenty-one Egyptian Christians on a Libyan beach by ISIS (2015). The examples could be multiplied many times over. I began writing this chapter on the day great numbers were slaughtered in three churches in Sri Lanka. To be slain in a church, once thought of as a sanctuary of safe refuge, recalls the assassination of two well-known archbishops, one in a cathedral, the other in a small chapel. On orders from the English king, Thomas Becket (d. 1170) was attacked in the cathedral of Canterbury by four knights and killed with a sword. Eight centuries later Archbishop Óscar Romero of San Salvador (d. 1980), who spoke out against poverty, social injustice, assassinations, and torture, was slain in a hospital chapel to silence his prophetic voice.

A widely-circulated reflection often attributed to Archbishop Romero, though actually composed by the late Bishop Kenneth Untener of Saginaw, Michigan, ends with the line "We are prophets of a future not our own." Such are modern day martyrs and prophets. Earlier in the reflection, Untener writes: "We plant the seeds that one day will grow. We water seeds already planted knowing that they hold future promise. We lay foundations that will need further development. We provide yeast that produces far beyond our capabilities."[19] In an often-quoted passage, Tertullian (d. ca. 230) underscored the multiplying effect of the blood of martyrs with seed imagery: "We multiply whenever we are mown down by you; the blood of Christians is seed" (*Apologeticus*, 50, s. 13). The testimony of the martyrs is extraordinary.

The scope of the so-called "Romero prayer" is not limited, however, to martyrs and prophets. It addresses all those who are faithful witnesses through word and deed to the living Christ. Few of us will ever be in situations where we face the choice between life and death because of our faith. Nonetheless, as members of the Body of Christ we are inseparably connected with those whose blood is shed for being a follower of Christ. We belong to them, and they to us. No matter what our circumstances in life, our trials and tribulations, we are called to be faithful witnesses. We are also called by Christ, in that magna carta of Christian living, the Sermon on the Mount, to pray for our persecutors and those who threaten Christians around the world (Matthew 5:44). It is a tall order. Yet it is one way that can transform our hearts and hopefully the hearts of those who cannot tolerate Christians in their midst.

For Reflection:

- In what situations have you found yourself when the commitment to live your faith has been placed in serious jeopardy?

- How do you witness to your faith at home, in the workplace, and in your community?

Chapter Seven

Death and Newness of Life in Paul's Eyes

A child's first memories of death leave an impact. When a beloved pet dies, or a dear family member passes away, a young person tries to make sense of such an event. I wonder what St. Paul's first experiences of death were and how these shaped him. I choose St. Paul because he towers above other apostles in the New Testament for his depth of reflection on life and death and also for the legacy of his letters. What did he learn from Rabbi Gamaliel, his likely instructor, about life and death in his religious tradition? How were the stories of Adam and Eve, Daniel, and the Maccabees presented? How did these shape his views of life and death?

Echoing language from the prophets, Paul believes that even before his birth God called him and by divine grace set him apart (Galatians 1:15). From his watershed experience on the road to Damascus, Paul announces the gospel with a remarkable religious fervor. His mission takes him from Damascus, to Jerusalem, to the metropolitan city of Antioch, through Asia Minor and Greece, with additional stops back in Jerusalem. Finally, he travels to Rome, the seat of the empire that dominated the Mediterranean (Acts 9—28), where he dies as a martyr.

In his first letter he is responding to the profound grief of the Thessalonians over those who have already died, possibly as a result of persecution in their city. He uses the metaphor "those who have fallen asleep" (1 Thessalonians 4:14, NABRE; "have died" in NRSV), suggesting that they will be awakened—as those who sleep ordinarily are—when the Lord returns. In expecting to be among the living at that time (4:15; compare 1 Corinthians 15:51), Paul is not claiming to be immortal, but rather that he will be among the saints who will experience transformation and then be fully united with Christ. As years pass and the intense expectation of the immediate return of the Messiah begins to wane, Paul realizes that he himself will face death (2 Corinthians 5:1-10; Philippians 1:21-22).

Today, Christians envision the parousia (the second coming of Christ) differently. Nonetheless, we all face the reality of death and its possible suddenness. Whether young or old, our personal return to God may happen at any moment. For this reason, St. Benedict reminds us to keep death daily before our eyes (Rule of Benedict 4,47) and St. Francis invites us to embrace death as he did, even praising God "through our Sister Death" (*Canticle of the Sun*). In doing this we engage ourselves fully in the richness of life, believing that when death comes we will see God face to face (Psalm 27:8).

Paul at Death's Door

Paul had many close calls with death. Often he risked his life in order to advance the gospel. Aware that there was a plot to kill him, Paul was lowered in a basket through an opening in the city wall (2 Corinthians 11:32-33; Acts 9:25). He endures countless floggings, receives thirty-nine lashes several times, is beaten with rods, is stoned, and is shipwrecked (2 Corinthians 11:23-25). On the one hand, he faces death with apprehension and despair; on the other, he longs for death with eagerness and anticipation (2 Corinthians 1:8-9; Philippians 1:20-26). In paradoxical language he experiences himself as dying, yet alive; "as punished, yet not killed" (2 Corinthians 6:9). Paul forcefully asserts "I die every day!" implying that he risked death daily. To emphasize the futility of belief in Christ without belief in the resurrection, he asks, "Why are we putting ourselves in danger every hour?" (1 Corinthians 15:30-31).

In the Letter to the Romans Paul answers his own query, explaining that he neither lives nor dies for the sake of himself. In other words, it is not about him! Rather, he lives for the sake of the Lord, and he dies for sake of the Lord. For this reason, he firmly attests that "we are the Lord's" (Romans 14:8).

To Live in Christ

Paul had a challenge on his hands when faced with the Corinthians, some of whom prided themselves on wisdom, others on being from wealthy and privileged families, and still others on their positions of power. Their personal status aside, Paul reminds them of their much more profound credentials, namely that God "is the source of your life in Christ Jesus" (1 Corinthians 1:30). Throughout his letters Paul speaks regularly of believers being "in Christ." The connection is so profound as to border on the mystical. To live one's life in Christ means on one level to be attuned to the mind of Christ, whose hallmarks are humility and selflessness (Philippians 2:3-11).

On a related level, to live in Christ means to be conformed to his death (Philippians 3:10). This happens through the realization that one's own sufferings are, from a faith perspective, a participation in the sufferings of Christ. The other day I had a conversation with Monica, an acquaintance I have known causally for over thirty years. She lives alone with her cat. She lost her husband four years ago in a freak accident, then lost her job, and now is losing her sight. She spends most of her time alone. She wonders: Why me? and What's next? As I listened to her I felt that her life is under the shadow of the "long loneliness" about which Dorothy Day speaks. A nominal Christian, perhaps someday, little by little, Monica will be given the grace to recover a sense of joy and to sense that her sufferings are in some mysterious way embraced by the one whose arms were stretched out on the cross.

Through Christ's death and resurrection, we have become a "new creation." One can imagine the exuberant Paul almost shouting: "Everything old has passed away;

see, everything has become new!" (2 Corinthians 5:17; also Galatians 6:15). Echoing God's proclamation through the prophet Isaiah—"For I am about to create new heavens / and a new earth" (65:17)—Paul announces that we have been re-fashioned, casting aside the old and putting on the new. Believers who live and move in Christ are a "new creation." Whatever has become tarnished, by wrong choices and sour moods, to the image of God in which we have been created has been fully restored in Christ. Through God's power and loving presence, we perceive in ways we have not noticed before the little signs and wonders unfolding before us and within us.

As we choose to live by that graced image, by that link between God and humans, we assist others in realizing that they too are made in God's image and can be clothed with the garment of new creation. Luke Timothy Johnson comments: "And when we regard and treat fellow humans as created in the image of God, things actually can change in the empirical realm; our fellow human being, now perceived as bearing a divine image and likeness, may respond like someone bearing such an impress."[20]

God has realized the new creation by reconciling us to God through Christ. That is just the beginning. Desiring the healing of a broken world, God has entrusted us with the ministry of reconciliation. Functioning as ambassadors for Christ—a role more esteemed than the highest-ranking officer in any diplomatic corps—we have a crucial part to play in the task of repairing the world, called *tikkun olam*, to borrow a central tenet of social justice from the Jewish tradition.

In the ancient world, reconciliation was used as a secular term to express the resolution of strained relationships between persons, peoples, and political foes. In these endeavors the offending party was expected to take the first step in restoring friendly relationships. Remarkably, Paul presents God, the aggrieved party, as the reconciler who takes the initiative. God, who is love, is not content with a fractured humanity, and hence is the first to act in restoring peace and harmony to troubled lives, indeed to the world at large.

The wellbeing and future of the whole cosmos, including all of life, is very much on Paul's mind in the much-celebrated eighth chapter of Romans, where he works out the implications of the new creation of 2 Corinthians 5:17. In Romans 8:18-25 creation is personified, longing to be set free from bondage and the suffering of death (which is traced back to the sin of Adam and Eve in Genesis chapter 3, as we saw earlier). Paul compares the travail of creation to the groaning pains suffered by a woman in labor. Once liberated, all creation will enjoy "the freedom of the glory of the children of God" (Romans 8:21). For the children of God this freedom will become manifest at the resurrection. As envisioned by Teilhard de Chardin, the renowned Jesuit devoted to understanding evolution, the entire universe is on an upward spiritual spiral toward the final reunification with the Divine. This could be thought of as human life writ large and may not be far off from Paul's sketch.

In the grand finale to Romans chapter 8, Paul expresses his conviction in hymnic jubilation that "neither death, nor life, nor angels, nor rulers, nor things present, nor things to come, nor powers ... nor anything else in all creation, will be able to separate us from the love of God in Christ Jesus our Lord" (8:38-39). Such is the wonder of God's life-giving power.

The Sentence of Death and the Mercy of God

For a moment, I would like to narrow our focus considerably to a subgroup of humanity which is discussed in connection with a statement by Paul later in his Letter to the Romans. This subgroup consists of those on death row. They live with the awareness that unless there is a last-minute stay of execution, their lives will be snatched away by the power of the state.

The passage in Romans that comes into play has been used to support capital punishment: "If you do what is wrong, you should be afraid, for the authority does not bear the sword in vain!" (13:4). Carrying the sword is a metaphor implying the power to punish, usually taken to mean execution. As a rationale for bearing the sword, Paul explains that the "servant of God" (referring here to the state) functions as an agent of punishment "to execute wrath on the wrongdoer" (Romans 13:5). In this controversial section on governing authorities (13:1-7), Paul reminds his audience that even though they are part of the new creation, this does not remove them from the exigencies of the existing political and social order.

Another biblical text cited in favor of the death penalty is Genesis 9:6: "Whoever sheds the blood of a human, / by a human shall that person's blood be shed" (see also Exodus 21:14; Numbers 35:31). Christian abolitionists of the death penalty argue that at no point does Jesus condone the death penalty. To the contrary, he abrogates the *lex talionis* (eye for an eye, tooth for a tooth, see Matthew 5:38-42), a principle which was, by the way, not about seeking revenge, but about ensuring that the punishment did not exceed the crime (Exodus 21:24). For Jesus the solution to injustice is not retribution but forgiveness (Matthew 18:21-22). Those against capital punishment also insist that all death, and hence all deliberate killing, is to be lamented because it strikes against human dignity and is an act of violence against the condemned person (and against the soul of the executioner).

Twenty states in the U.S. and more than two-thirds of countries worldwide have abolished the death penalty, once referred to by Supreme Count Justice Harry Blackman as the "machinery of death."[21] It remains incumbent upon governments, however, to provide for the security and safety of society, diligently protecting its citizens from threats to life and acts of violence.

Jesus himself suffered the death penalty, executed on the cross between two criminals. Thus, through the manner of his own death, he was closely identified with all those who experienced a similar fate. Up until recently the traditional teaching of the Catholic Church upheld "the right and duty of legitimate public authority to punish malefactors by ... the death penalty" (*CCC*, 2266). Pope Francis drew a mixed response when he fully reversed this position in a pronouncement in February 2018, affirming that now "the Church teaches, in the light of the Gospel, that 'the death penalty is inadmissible because it is an attack on the inviolability and dignity of the person.'"[22]

Before Pope Francis, others have passionately argued against the death penalty. These include, notably, Sister Helen Prejean who for years has brought to those condemned a warm smile and a caring presence that lifted their spirits before life was forced from their restrained flesh. Others, like Bryan Stevenson, an attorney, work tirelessly to defend those on death row, some of whom have been wrongly convicted.[23] The execution of the innocent is an injustice that can never be reversed.

From Life to Life

One wonders whether anyone was there to support, to encourage, and to pray with Paul before he was executed during the reign of Nero. Did he see his impending death as the ultimate and final way to imitate Jesus (1 Corinthians 11:1)? From his letters we know that he evaluated his entire life in light of Jesus' death on the cross and his resurrection. This is what gave him meaning and purpose, empowering him to "walk in newness of life" (Romans 6:4). The bodily self where sin once held sway is the same body where the newness of life manifests itself. Through Christ believers are to present themselves "to God as those who have been brought from death to life" (Romans 6:13). Yet, always confident, walking by faith and not by sight, Paul preferred to "be away from the body and at home with the Lord" (2 Corinthians 5:8).

He identified himself and other believers as the aroma of the Anointed One, "a fragrance from life to life" (2 Corinthians 2:16). This expression is a rhetorical flourish to impress upon his hearers that the reception of the gospel meant for them life and not death. Yet the paradox of Christian faith is evident in Paul's ministry, for he believed that he always carried "in the body the death of Jesus, so that the life of Jesus may also be made visible" in his body (2 Corinthians 4:10).

Paul interpreted his own sufferings as parallel to those of Jesus. But he knew and believed that Jesus, who suffered and died, also rose. Through his profound identification with Jesus Messiah, Paul becomes a model himself for all believers to embrace their own sufferings, and the daily dying to self, as they aspire to live a life of authenticity and eventually to "reap eternal life from the Spirit" (Galatians 6:8). For Paul an authentic life is one of freedom measured by love for one another. Thus believers are to live by the Spirit and be guided by the Spirit, yielding fruits of love, joy, and peace among the rich harvest that manifests newness of life (Galatians 5:13-26).

For Reflection:

- What does it mean to you to be united to the person of Christ? How do you imitate Christ in your daily life?

- If you faced the choice now to remain at home in the body, i.e., to continue living on planet earth, or to be with the Lord in the afterlife, which would you choose?

Chapter Eight

Living Well and Dying Well

"These past two months have felt like God's grace is upon us. So many blessings have come our way," Sophia shared with a lightened heart, in response to the overwhelming support she received from friends and colleagues. For the past year she had been faithfully accompanying her husband Kevin who was battling metastatic cancer. Then, they made the bold decision to go on a cruise to celebrate their thirty-fifth wedding anniversary. Sophia reflects: "The food was great and we loved being at sea. It was all life-giving! Kevin and I returned with a new view on life and living. He said, 'There is life and there is living. We choose to live.' The trip helped us step out of our intense story into life, culture, beauty, and music. We shared wonderful moments together as we walked through ancient ruins, historic places, and beautiful scenery."

Faced with the ups and downs of a life-threatening illness, this couple embraced life, aware that their time together was now compressed into a few months, perhaps a year. The twin themes of blessing and gratitude emerge as their way of celebrating life.

The person of faith, aware that all of life is a gift, joins voices with the psalmist: "Bless the LORD, O my soul, / and all that is within me, / bless his holy name" (Psalm 103:1). The Divine is blessed for being merciful and gracious, slow to anger, abounding in steadfast love, and compassionate. Blessings flow from a spirit of gratitude.

Sometimes experiences of gratitude come in bunches. Within the span of thirty minutes this Sunday morning, I witnessed three. A good friend facing many medical complications this past year shared that his bilirubin levels dropped to a level low enough to be included in a clinical trial. He referred to this little change as the hoped-for mustard seed. He had just learned this good news from the nurse practitioner, Gabriel, whom he knew was aptly named after the biblical messenger of glad tidings (Luke 1:19). Just before that, an artistic homebound person to whom I have been bringing the Eucharist shared his gratitude that he had recovered sufficiently from a series of surgeries to begin painting again. When I arrived, he was exuberant, listening to chants composed by Hildegard of Bingen. Then I read an article reprinted in *America* magazine by a registered nurse, who though devastated at the death of her eight-year-old son, thanked God daily for letting her be with him when he died, an experience that removed her own fears and uncertainties about death.

Blessings and Gratitude

Final blessings are often given and received at the end of life. In a biblical account that combines charming comedy and trickery, Isaac unwittingly gives his blessing to his younger son Jacob, who masqueraded as Esau, the father's older and favorite son (Genesis 27:1-45). Later Jacob wrestles with a divine being—a favorite story of struggle with the supernatural—and does not let go until the angel blesses him (Genesis 32:26). On receiving the blessing he is renamed Israel, which later becomes the name of his people. At the end of his life, Israel blesses Joseph's two sons Ephraim and Manasseh, his own son Joseph, and then all his sons, offering commendation to some of them and—surely to their utter shock—condemnation to others (Genesis 48:8-14, 49:1-28).

Blessings given at life's end bring closure for the dying, confer God's favor, and express hopes of wellbeing for the next generation, setting them on a course of living well. How tragic when one's final words come as condemnation, as Israel pronounced on some of his sons, or today, when an angry parent disowns a son or daughter even up to death. One of the greatest gifts a community can offer to its members, a friend to a dear companion, or parents to their children is one's blessing, for such are "stronger than the blessings of the eternal mountains" (Genesis 49:26).

Sophia and Kevin "felt like God's grace is upon" them. Their hearts were filled with gratitude. To cultivate the daily discipline of gratitude enlarges our sense of blessings received. So much of what we enjoy comes as a gift, a modest act of kindness from a neighbor, a warm hug from our child in the midst of play, a gentle touch on the shoulder from a dear friend.

The psalmists sensed deep within their spirits the bounty of the Divine, joyfully acclaiming: "I will give thanks to the LORD with my whole heart" (Psalm 9:1), and acknowledging the beneficence of the Creator: "*Give thanks to the LORD, for he is good*" (Psalm 136:1). To wake up with the sense of gratitude for another day aware that "this is the day that the LORD has made" gives us every reason to "rejoice and be glad in it" (Psalm 118:24). Gratitude directed to God and shared with one another creates joy in us, and so fills our life.

How easy it is for us to become grateful for all the good things that come our way. Yet many are the days filled with painful moments that create bad memories. We regret the latter, wanting to banish them from our thoughts, but hold onto and treasure the former. Gratitude is not about slicing up our life into the good and the bad. It is about reclaiming our entire past and seeing even in our disappointments and betrayals, rejections and misdeeds "the pruning hands of God purifying my heart for deeper love, stronger hope, and broader hope," as Henri Nouwen reflects. Grateful are those, he adds, "who can celebrate even the pains of life because they trust that when harvest time comes the fruit will show that the pruning was not punishment but purification."[24] The call to gratitude is to see that all is grace, even the shadows and the darkness.

How difficult it can be when, in the words of the psalmist, "my companions ... shun me" (Psalm 88:8), or when "even my bosom friend in whom I trusted / ... has lifted the heel against me" (Psalm 41:9). Or take the case of those in positions of authority over us, just as the historical Pontius Pilate controlled the destiny of Jesus. Our Pilates may have closed doors we aspired to walk through, worked against us, or dashed our dreams.[25]

In my case, I think of a general manager of a health care institution who abruptly ended what seemed like a very fine and thriving CPE program that I and a colleague had built up over the years. How hard it is to resist harboring vengeful feelings toward the Pilates in our experience, and even more difficult—at least in the moment—to move forward in hope trusting that God will lead us to new, life-giving experiences. Yet, with such painful pruning, might we not in time see new growth, and for that earlier opposition actually be grateful? About the foundation of our hope, Paul reminds us: "In all these things we are more than conquerors through him who loved us" (Romans 8:37).

Expressing gratitude, even by simply saying thank you, is part of the larger woven fabric of utterances that continually shape a life well lived. We turn again to the life of Jesus to listen closely to his "sacrament of speech."[26] For the thief crucified on the cross next to him, Jesus not only heard his wish to be remembered—a nearly universal aspiration of the dying—but offered him much more, a homecoming beyond anything he could imagine (Luke 23:39-43). "You will be with me in Paradise"! In the parable of the prodigal son there is also a welcoming home of two problematic sons, the estranged one who had left home in search of the good life, the other who stayed home nursing grudges. The merciful father extends forgiveness and makes plans to celebrate and rejoice (Luke 15:11-32).

Offering Forgiveness

The forgiveness theme also emanates from the suffering, dying Jesus. He asked his Father to forgive those who crucified him (Luke 23:34), implying that he himself had already done so. I forgive you! Being without sin, there is no record that Jesus himself asked for pardon. Yet, it would not be totally surprising had he simply said, "I'm sorry," to the Canaanite woman whom Matthew reports Jesus treated rather rudely (Matthew 15:21-28). Jesus instructs us to pray: "And forgive us our sins, / for we ourselves forgive everyone indebted to us" (Luke 11:4).

At the very beginning of Jesus' long goodbye to the disciples, commonly known as his farewell address (John chapters 13—17), the evangelist accentuates Jesus' enduring and deep love for the disciples: "he loved them to the end" (John 13:1). I love you! What about gratitude? The Gospels stress that Jesus lived in thankfulness to his Father (Luke 10:21; John 11:41). I thank you! Although the sacred texts do not mention this—they only contain a small portion of the Jesus tradition—Jesus undoubtedly would have expressed thanks, or at least felt grateful, to those close to him, for example, to the women and the Twelve who accompanied him through cities and villages (Luke 8:1-3), to Martha and Mary who welcomed him as their dinner guest (Luke 10:38-42), and to his mother and the other women for their unwavering support as they stood near the cross (John 19:25-27).

Reminiscent of the simple, yet profound sacraments of speech from the Jesus tradition, Ira Byock, a palliative care physician, names four words that matter most in nurturing and mending relationships: "Please forgive me," "I forgive you," "Thank you," and "I love you."[27] When said from the heart these words can free a person from toxic emotions of anger, bitterness, and spiritual pain. In working with patients at the end of their life, Byock found that these were the most meaningful heartfelt words that could help bring healing to fractured relationships and reconciliation with loved ones.

When the course of life reaches its end, closure with loved ones becomes a prime factor. How often a dying parent holds on, often to the amazement of medical staff, until the absent son or daughter arrives at the bedside. Saying that final "goodbye" brings release and the ability to let go. This is a sacred time to share what is still left unsaid. To listen with the heart is to be attentive to the quiet space between the words, and to be open to the presence of the Divine in the I-Thou moments that the Jewish theologian Martin Buber speaks about. Although such moments may be tearful and emotionally draining, they can bring peace of heart. With hands held, there is the warm imprint of imminent departure, separation, and "I will miss you."

Linguists explain that the farewell "goodbye" originated as a contracted form of "God be with you." When this religious nuance comes into play, the underlying belief is that departing loved ones (whether they are simply traveling home or leaving this life behind entirely) do not make that journey alone. For the Creator who has been there from the beginning accompanies the dying on the most significant part of their life journey, through the darkness of death to life beyond. To die well is to rely fully on God's good nature and to mutually exchange the wish for God to be with both the dying and those who remain.

God's Presence and Power through the Sacraments

For believers, the presence of God is powerfully symbolized through the sacraments. The sacrament of reconciliation provides forgiveness and restores any rupture in the friendship with God and one another. It brings the same peace that the risen Christ imparted to the fearful disciples when he said: "Peace be with you" (John 20:19, 21, 26). The Letter of James gives instructions about the benefit of the sacrament of anointing of the sick. Unabashedly, James teaches that the anointing with oil is powerful and effective: "that you may be healed" (James 5:16). There have been instances of physical healing, or improvement in patients' conditions, although most often the effect is spiritual.

Once I witnessed what can only be called a miraculous healing. David was a young man whose injuries were so severe the doctors offered no hope. But he received the sacrament and recovered, astounding everyone. A newspaper story erroneously reported that David "defied" the "Last Rites." Rather, a faith perspective would hold that the "Last Rites" were instrumental in his healing. Through anointing the sick are promised divine help. Laying hands on the person and anointing the forehead, the minister prays: "Through this holy anointing may the Lord in his love and mercy help you with the grace of the Holy Spirit." Often there is a visible decrease in anxiety and a movement toward inner calm as the person is commended to the Creator.

The third sacrament given to the dying is the Eucharist, called in this instance Viaticum, literally, "food for the journey." Receiving the risen Lord in Communion assures the dying that she participates in the death of Christ and through her sufferings will soon be united with the resurrection of Christ. Moreover, taking part regularly in the Eucharistic liturgy throughout one's life provides the spiritual strength to live faithfully as a Christian. The Eucharist itself is the supreme act of thanksgiving (the Greek meaning of the term) by which the faithful express gratitude to God for all that has been accomplished through creation, redemption, and sanctification (CCC, 360). Nourished by the Eucharist on Sunday, the Lord's Day, the faithful are entrusted to live out the gospel values the rest of the week, both at work and at home. At the end of Mass we are instructed to "Go in peace," sometimes with the added instruction, "glorifying the Lord by your life."

The Church has a long tradition of supporting the faithful to die well. This reached a crisis point during the Black Plague (1347-1351) when up to one-third of the European population died, some within a few days of contracting the disease. With insufficient clergy to attend to the dying—many priests also succumbed—there developed the *ars moriendi* (art of dying) tradition. Pamphlets were widely distributed with detailed block cut images and brief commentary alerting the dying to the five temptations they were likely to experience and reminding them about the powerful spiritual resources available to assist them in resisting these pitfalls as they prepared to meet their Creator.

Portrayed with vivid imagery of the competing forces of the devil and his minions on one side of the death bed, and the saints, the Virgin, and Christ on the other, the dying were able to grasp in one glance the spiritual drama their soul may be facing. The big five temptations that arise are doubt and loss of faith, despair, avarice, impatience, and complacency. To fight these the dying had five spiritual weapons to draw upon: faith, hope, charity, patience, and humility.

There have been a number of endeavors to transpose the traditional *ars moriendi* into a modern key to address the contemporary scene, both religious and secular.[28] One approach is biblically inspired, lifting up Jesus' virtues of patience, hope, and compassion as exemplified in Luke's Passion narrative. Jesus manifested patience in the face of his agony in the Garden of Gethsemane, hope in relying on God to remain with him during his trials, and compassion toward the wayward disciple Peter.[29]

Another approach adds to the five virtues mentioned above those of letting go, serenity, gratitude, and courage.[30]

The first implies a letting go of tightfisted grasping driven by egocentric anxiety. From this comes serenity that the dying remain in the good care of God, confident they are upheld by God's power and grace. Out of such confidence flows gratitude to God. The final virtue is to face death with courage, poignantly displayed by letting go. Courage is founded firmly on the belief that death does not have the last word. This was demonstrated powerfully and definitively by God who raised Jesus from the dead. To that event we now turn.

For Reflection:

- What adaptations would you like to make to your daily routine in order to enhance your enjoyment of life?

- What would a good death look like for you? How can you best prepare for this?

Chapter Nine

Christ Risen to New Life

"The most shocking event in human history," is how Pope Francis rates the resurrection of Jesus, the Galilean peasant, in his Easter message on April 22, 2019.[31] Yet, in another list of the top fifty shocking historical happenings—where 9/11 and the Holocaust rank first and second respectively—the resurrection does not even make the cut.[32] Apart from whatever bias such surveys may reflect, it must be noted that if the followers of Jesus did not have an experience of the risen Jesus, then Christianity as a global religion—and its massive impact on world history—would not exist.

Nonetheless, some people struggle with Easter because they find it difficult to believe that Jesus rose from the dead. Others profess that the resurrection is not about the empty tomb but about the after-effect of a shared memory of the historical Jesus or a more spiritualized belief that love is stronger than life or death. The Jesuit priest and popular author James Martin counters that *Jesus' resurrection is not "any sort of parable or metaphor," but rather means* "that Jesus Christ rose from the dead on the first Easter Sunday."[33] Only a profound experience with the risen Lord explains the remarkable change the disciples underwent from being frightened in the upper room to boldly proclaiming that Jesus lives.

Writing to the Corinthians, Paul addresses some skeptics who in his own time denied the resurrection of Jesus: "If Christ has not been raised, then our proclamation has been in vain and your faith has been in vain" (1 Corinthians 15:14). Then, he ups the ante with this argument: "If for this life only we have hoped in Christ, we are of all people most to be pitied" (15:19). If there is no risen Christ, then Paul and other believers would be betting their lives on a fantasy with no grounding in reality. This recalls the response he received when preaching to the Athenians (Acts 17:32), who scoffed at him since Christ's resurrection made no sense in light of the Hellenistic doctrine of the soul. Such scoffing echoes down through history, including some Christians who doubt, or outright deny, the resurrection.[34]

Belief in resurrection emerged gradually in the Old Testament before the rise of Christianity. In a remarkable passage, the prophet Ezekiel has a vision of dry bones which the Lord God brought to life by restoring their flesh and breathing into them the breath of life (Ezekiel chapter 37). This passage is not about the resurrection of the individual, but rather the restoration of the "whole house of Israel," after the exile in Babylon (37:11). As we have already seen, the first clear witness to the resurrection of the dead occurs in Daniel 12:1-3, where at the end of time "many [not all] of those who sleep in the dust of the earth shall awake, some to everlasting life, and some to shame" (punishment).

No text speaks about the resurrection in history of a separate individual. Thus, Jesus' resurrection, even as Messiah, would never have been expected in Judaism.

In the New Testament era, the Pharisees, a major religious group of devout laity within Judaism who were devoted to the study of the Law, believed in the resurrection, a belief that would have been well known to both Jesus and Paul, himself a Pharisee. The Sadducees, a party of high priests and aristocrats, denied the resurrection. Neither group would have believed in the resurrection of Messiah Jesus.

Early Preaching of the Resurrection of Christ

How did the first Christians preach the resurrection of Christ? The shortest version is found in the earliest Christian writing (dated around 51 A.D.), where Paul reminds the Thessalonians that the "living and true God ... raised from the dead—Jesus," a belief that he reiterates in chapter four of the letter: "we believe that Jesus died and rose again" (1 Thessalonians 1:9-10, 4:14). A few years later the apostle relates a more expanded version of a "credal statement" that he had received: "that Christ died for our sins in accordance with the scriptures, and that he was buried, and that he was raised on the third day in accordance with the scriptures" (1 Corinthians 15:3-4).

The last passage cited contains three important elements with crucial interpretative comments. The first is that

Jesus' death had profound salvific significance: it brought about atonement by the forgiveness of sins. "The scriptures" may refer to the Suffering Servant songs in Isaiah (42:1-4, 49:1-6, 50:4-9, 52:13—53:12). Proof of Jesus' death—also demonstrated by the soldier who pierced his side (John 19:34)—is confirmed by the fact of his burial. His being raised according to the scriptures possibly alludes to the prophetic texts which mention the third day (Hosea 6:2; Jonah 1:17; see Mark 8:31).

To any skeptics, Paul says that you can confirm his assertion by contacting those to whom the risen Jesus appeared, including Peter and the Twelve, the "more than five hundred" believers—many of whom, Paul notes, are still alive (some twenty years after the event)—and the other apostles. Without going into details Paul also asserts that Jesus appeared to him as well. For reasons unknown, Paul does not mention any woman in the list of witnesses, not even Mary Magdalene who, as we will see from the Gospel tradition, was the first to announce the risen Christ to the apostles.

Paul's four main points could not be more concise: Jesus died, was buried, was raised, and appeared. The Gospels amplify each of these occurrences in narrative form. The story they tell regarding Jesus' death is truly shocking; the story they tell regarding his resurrection is truly amazing. Equally stunning is this assessment that came not from any of the disciples who struggled to believe but from a Roman centurion and his contingent: "Truly this man was God's Son!" (Matthew 27:54).

The resurrection can only be understood in the context of the cross. For Paul "the cross is foolishness to those who are perishing" (1 Corinthians 1:18). Yes, but it is much more than that. This deeply ingrained symbol of the Christian tradition represents the most excruciating form of capital punishment meted out by the Romans to those who challenged their rule and disrupted order. When he was condemned to death, Jesus experienced the inhumane treatment of a convicted criminal: he was flogged, stripped of his garments, then nailed to a cross (others were simply tied). Then the crucified was displayed in a prominent public place as a deterrent for all passersby against insubordination to imperial power. One might pause a bit, before heaping blame on the faint-hearted disciples for deserting Jesus at his arrest and "getting out of Dodge" (Mark 14:50), for fearing that after the Romans captured Jesus, they would be next.

The Empty Tomb and the Appearances of the Risen Christ in the Gospels

I invite the reader to follow closely with me the biblical accounts of the resurrection of Jesus—so fundamental to our faith—looking first at the account in Mark (the earliest Gospel), then those in Matthew and Luke who augment Mark's account. According to Mark, three faithful women who had witnessed Jesus' death—Mary Magdalene, Mary the mother of James, and Salome—went to his tomb after the Sabbath to anoint his body. Almost as an afterthought, they realized they had not planned how they would gain access to the sealed tomb. Then, to their astonishment, they not only saw that the tomb had been opened but also that a young man clothed in white was standing inside. This messenger from God interpreted for them the empty tomb: "He has been raised; he is not here" (Mark 16:6; recall 1 Corinthians 15:3-4). The angel then tells them to instruct the disciples to go to Galilee, where they will see Jesus.

In no Gospel account is the empty tomb itself the basis for belief. Nor does anyone actually witness Jesus rising from the dead. Rather, it is the proclamation of another— He is risen!—that leads to faith. Even though the women in Mark fled the tomb in "terror and amazement" and "said nothing to anyone" (Mark 16:8), they now know that Jesus lives; he is no longer confined to the realm of the dead. Death does not have the last word, for God, who so often had rescued Israel from death, has raised up Jesus to new life. (The *Exsultet* sung at the Easter Vigil dramatically links God's deliverance of Israel and of Jesus.) In the other Gospels, personal encounters with the risen Jesus confirm for the women and the disciples that he is alive.

The resurrection narrative in the Gospel of Matthew addresses questions left unanswered by Mark. Matthew explains that "a great earthquake" caused the stone to roll away (Matthew 28:2). Also, he places guards on the scene, preempting an alternative explanation for the empty tomb, namely that someone stole the body. Matthew also adds an account of Jesus' appearance, and this was to the two Marys who hear from Jesus: "Greetings!" (28:9). There are two parallel scenes after the visit to the tomb, one laudatory, the other deceitful. In the former the women are instructed not to be afraid (a corrective to Mark 16:8?) and to tell the disciples that they will see the risen Jesus in Galilee. In the latter, the guards accept a bribe to spread the false account that the disciples stole Jesus' body at night while they were sleeping (!). In addition, Matthew does not leave the women silent, but relates that they joyfully ran to tell the disciples.

Finally, with the Great Commission, the denouement of the Easter events, the risen Christ solemnly assures the believers of his enduring presence: "And remember, I am with you always, to the end of the age" (Matthew 28:20). There have been times in the history of the Church when this promise seems to have been severely tested, during such dark periods as the Inquisition, the corrupt papacies, and, in our age, the sex abuse crisis among the clergy. Yet, despite these scandals, the Spirit of the risen Christ remains at work leading the Church forward on its true mission.

Especially touching and endearing are the resurrection accounts in the Gospels of Luke and John. In Luke two men, later identified as angels (Luke 24:23), give a crystal-clear message to the startled women who come to the tomb, asking them, "Why do you look for the living among the dead?" (Luke 24:5). Their dazzling clothes recall the Transfiguration, when the clothes of Jesus becoming dazzling white (Luke 9:28-36). Also in Luke, the women remember what Jesus told them when he was still in Galilee: "the Son of Man must be handed over to sinners, and be crucified, and on the third day rise again" (Luke 24:6-7).

In a passage marked by irony, Luke narrates a surprise encounter with the risen Christ, who, in the guise of an unknown traveler, approaches two forlorn disciples—perhaps husband and wife—their hopes dashed by the death of the Messiah, Jesus. Then when this stranger breaks bread with them at table in the village of Emmaus "their eyes were opened, and they recognized him." Even more, they realized "our hearts [were] burning within us" while he walked with them on the road (Luke 24:31-32). "The breaking of bread" is Luke's phrase for the celebration of the Lord's Supper (see Acts 2:42). Like the two disciples of Emmaus we are Easter people walking with the risen Christ who transforms our lives, often in unexpected ways.

Each Sunday when the worshipping community gathers around the table of the Lord, the sacred presence of the Risen One is experienced among us and within our hearts. The experience of this powerful presence is only possible because Jesus—no longer constrained by his earthly existence—lives among us. Through Christ, the life-giving spirit, personal transformation takes place, a deep sense of solidarity is felt, and resurrection faith is celebrated.

The Resurrection of Christ in the Gospel of John and in Paul

In the Gospel of John blood and water came forth from Jesus on the cross when one of the soldiers pierced his side

(John 19:34). These elements symbolize the sacraments of Eucharist and baptism. John also tells of the disciple Thomas, who did not believe Jesus had risen until he touched the wounds of Jesus and put his hand in his side. This he did a week after Jesus rose. In doing so, he came to believe not only in the risen Jesus, but also that he was Lord (John 20:28). As the German theologian Gerhard Lohfink has astutely pointed out, the historicity of the appearance accounts in the Gospels is not to be denied, since they radically changed the attitude of the fleeing disciples from fear and doubt to belief and courage.[35]

Before the Thomas episode, John tells the intimate story of Mary Magdalene weeping at the tomb. When Jesus appeared to her—totally unexpected—she mistakes him for the gardener, until the moment of recognition. Then in a very tender passage, he calls her by name, "Mary," and she responds "Rabbouni!" (meaning Teacher, John 20:16). So drawn to him, she reaches out to hold on to him, but Jesus explains he has to ascend to the Father first. Then Mary Magdalene announces to the male disciples, "I have seen the Lord" (John 20:18). Note that in all the Gospels, women, not the male apostles or even Peter, their head, are the first to announce the resurrection. How fitting that Mary Magdalene—whose memorial was elevated to a feast day (July 22) by Pope Francis in 2016—has been referred to as the Apostle of the Resurrection or the Apostle to the Apostles. The full implications of her role and that of the other female proclaimers to the disciples have yet to be fully realized for women in our contemporary Church.

Paul further develops the status of the risen Christ. Having been raised by God, Christ is seated at God's right hand (Romans 8:34). As portrayed in an early Christian hymn that Paul draws upon (Colossians 1:15-20), Christ is praised and exalted as the head of all things and specifically the head of the body, identified with the Church. The supremacy of Christ has a cosmic dimension. The risen Christ rules over everything we experience on earth and everything in the vast expanse of the heavens, both visible and invisible. Although our lives may seem fragmented at times and nations seem to be more in conflict with each other rather than working together for peace, Christ is the one in whom "all things hold together" (verse 17).

As the firstborn from the dead, Christ stands at the origin of the resurrection, thus assuring us that we, whose lives are marked by love and fidelity, will rise with him. Already now believers, having died with Christ through baptism, are secure in Christ. He draws all of us to himself.

This lofty hymn in Colossians which praises the role of the risen Christ is read on the feast of Christ the King, instituted by Pope Pius XI in 1925 in response to growing secularism. For the most part we no longer live in a world of kings, but we are very aware of the powerful people who tend to dominate others with minimal regard for human dignity or the common good. This hymn reminds us not to lose heart, for the source of our confidence is the risen Christ in whom "all the fullness of God was pleased to dwell" (1:19).

For Reflection

- How do you experience the presence of the risen Christ in your everyday life? What have been your Emmaus experiences?

- In what ways does the Church need to continually be reformed so that it more closely conforms to the risen Christ?

Chapter Ten

The Resurrection of the Dead

The first stop in our discussion of the resurrection of the dead is at the cemetery. The diversity of views expressed on tombstones reminds us of the span of perspectives in the Bible, though they may not match. The psalmist blatantly states, "Fools say in their hearts, 'There is no God'" (Psalm 14:1). Yet, one epitaph claims to be predictive: "See? Told you there is no god." Another comes across as wry humor: "All dressed up and no place to go." Then there are the humorous ones that do not commit regarding an afterlife: "See, I told you I was sick" and "Here lies John Yeast, pardon me for not rising" (humor only, or conviction too?).

A proverbial tone is struck with this common inscription: "Remember friend as you pass by / As you are now, so once was I / As I am now, soon you may be / Prepare for death and follow me." Then there are those where faith is evident: "Blessed are the pure in heart, for they will see God" (Matthew 5:8) and "And I shall dwell in the house of the Lord forever" (Psalm 23:6). In the catacombs outside of Rome—where thousands of early Christians were buried beginning in the second century—the great majority of Christian inscriptions read

"*In Pace*" (In Peace), meaning essentially, "I am at peace because I know where I am going after I die," namely, to their Savior who promised lasting peace.[36]

The peace given by the Johannine Jesus both before and after his death (John 14:27, 20:19-21) is a hallmark of eternal life with God. The resurrection itself is grounded in the identity of God. As we have already seen in Daniel and Second Maccabees, God, who is imminently just, vindicates the righteous who suffer and are put to death. The preeminent act of God's justice is expressed in raising Jesus after he was put to death in the cruelest manner, though he was completely innocent. In the resurrection accounts the women at the tomb and the larger group of disciples profoundly experienced the risen Christ, empowering them to proclaim the saving effect of his death and resurrection.

The early Church was fully aware that Christ's resurrection was not an isolated event. Rather this momentous event marked a new beginning and served as the model of how God would act on behalf of all who believed. Jesus is not just the "Author of life, whom God raised from the dead" (Acts 3:15); he is also "the first fruits" of the resurrection harvest (1 Corinthians 15:20,23), "the firstborn within a large family" (Romans 8:29), and "the firstborn from the dead" (Colossians 1:18; Revelation 1:5). As the first fruits of the harvest and the firstborn of the dead, the risen Jesus becomes the pattern for all. He is the beginning of the resurrection of all the dead.

Christ the First Fruits

With Jesus being the first to rise from the dead, what about Lazarus? Was his "raising" from the dead in the Fourth Gospel part of the anticipated full harvest (John 11:44)? Martha was stricken with grief because her brother, whom Jesus loved, died before Jesus arrived on the scene. Jesus' promise, "Your brother will rise again" (11:23), appeared to offer little reassurance in the moment. Jesus himself became "greatly disturbed in spirit and deeply moved" and he began to weep (11:33, 35). He responded by thanking the Father and crying out in a loud voice, "Lazarus, come out!" (11:43). The dead man Lazarus comes out; the bindings and strips of cloth— the trappings of death— are removed. In this narrative Lazarus is restored to his earthly life and not transformed into a "spiritual body." Strictly speaking this is not a story of resurrection from the dead, but one of resuscitation, that is, revival from "death" and restoration to physical life.

This brings us to Paul, for whom the expression "resurrection of the dead" refers to all the dead (plural), not just to an individual. This means that the ultimate destiny of life with God encompasses all humanity, and as we said earlier, even all creation. Traditionally this has been understood as happening at the general resurrection of the dead at the end of time. Since with death time as we know it ceases, to speak about some "intermediate state" between one's individual death and the final resurrection confines the person after death to the temporal limits that mark change in the material world.

With death there is reckoning in the presence of God by Christ Jesus "who is to judge the living and the dead" (2 Timothy 4:1). The divine accounting is poignantly laid out in Matthew 25:31-46, often referred to as the final exam for Christians. The criteria for evaluation are concrete: Were the works of mercy demonstrated in one's earthly pilgrimage? The result is eternal life for those who cared for the least of their brothers and sisters and eternal punishment for those who did not. Inextricable from this judgment is the emphasis on divine mercy celebrated on the Second Sunday of Easter. This reflects Paul's belief in a God "who is rich in mercy" (Ephesians 2:4). Whether there is universal salvation so that even those who did great evil are ultimately forgiven continues to be hotly debated. The Catholic Church prays "that no one should be lost," desiring everyone to be saved (*CCC*, 1058; see also 1821, with reference to 1 Timothy 2:4).

Taking a closer look at salvation, we turn to Paul's extensive, artfully crafted discussion of the resurrection of Christians in 1 Corinthians 15:35-58 where he discusses the nature of our risen existence, and more specifically the resurrection of the body. This section is set up by two questions from an interlocutor in verse 35: "How are the dead raised? With what kind of body do they come?" Whether these queries are to be taken seriously or sardonically brought forth by a skeptic is hard to say. In verses 36-49 Paul uses multiple antitheses to contrast the present mortal body with the incorruptible future body of the resurrection. In verses 50-58 he focuses on the dramatic transformation of the body at the resurrection.

Among the notable contemporary thinkers with whom Paul would have an engaging discussion is the late Harvard professor and scientific genius Stephen Hawking (d. 2019). He rejected an afterlife, asserting: "I regard the brain as a computer which will stop working when its components fail. There is no heaven or afterlife for broken down computers; that is a fairy story for people afraid of the dark."[37] Commenting enigmatically that "knowing the mind of God is knowing the laws of nature,"[38] he was adamant that he did not believe in God or the resurrection.

The Resurrection of Our Mortal Body

Paul argues in 1 Corinthians 15:36-38 that there can be no resurrection without prior death. To illustrate this point, he appeals to botany: a bare seed must be sown before a plant is produced. In this analogy he identifies the seed that is sown with the mortal body. Then, he introduces a theological argument, stating that God gives the seed its particular body as God so chooses. The point of the analogy is that a seed must lose its old form to become a new flowering plant. So too the resurrection of the body will bear little resemblance to the dead physical body.

Paul urges the reader to look around and notice the diversity of flesh, pointing to different living beings: animals, birds, and fish. This evokes the first Creation account in Genesis. He follows this by drawing distinctions between earthly and heavenly bodies (sun, moon, and stars), each with its own unique glory (15:39-41). The ancients, including Plato, believed that the stars were living beings divine and everlasting. The multiple recurrences of the Greek word *soma* (body) in these verses suggest that Paul is thinking of the human body, which, through resurrection, will become a spiritual body with its own glory.

Paul is building his argument for the resurrection of the body, thus emphasizing that the afterlife involves more than a nebulous, disembodied spirit. In verses 42-49 Paul returns to the seed analogy and applies it to the resurrection of the dead. What is sown, that is, the mortal physical body, will be raised with radically new characteristics: it is raised imperishable, in glory, in power, and a spiritual body.

Let's pause here to ponder our bodily nature. Through our bodies we participate in the material world around us, and on a larger scale are part of the entire cosmos. The main elements making up 97% of our physical being—hydrogen, carbon, nitrogen, and oxygen—are also found in the stars near and far. These elements have a cosmic history we are born into, interact through metabolic processes with our immediate environment during our earthly life, and will continue in some fashion after our death. Through our bodies we relate to our environment, form relationships, and experience change. By breathing, drinking, and eating, we take in matter that then becomes part of who we are. On a spiritual level, the love we experience, our dreams, our goals, and our aspirations come to expression in and through our bodies. Through our bodies and our memories, we develop our identity from the earliest period of our life until our last day.[39]

Thanks to neuroscience we now know that spiritual and religious practices whereby we relate to God have measurable effects on the brain. Andrew Newberg, professor of neuroscience, has shown that "meditating Buddhists and praying Catholic nuns, for instance, have increased activity in the frontal lobes of the brain."[40] The religious and mystical experience registered on the brain seems to confirm an intimate connection between the material and the spiritual. At the resurrection the former is transformed into the latter, as Paul articulates: "It [our mortal body] is sown a physical body, it [our mortal body] is raised a spiritual body" (1 Corinthians 15:44). Hence, the resurrection of the dead will mean, as Gerald O'Collins explains, "the full and final personalizing and spiritualizing of our matter, not its abolition."[41]

Continuing with Paul's narrative, we come upon his ingenious midrash (commentary) on the Creation account of the first human in Genesis 2:7. He contrasts the second/last Adam with the first Adam. Whereas "'The first man, Adam, became a living being'; the last Adam became a life-giving spirit" (15:45). It is precisely the last Adam, the risen Christ, who is the source of life for the resurrected body. Paul contrasts the origins of the two Adams: the first is from the earth and the second is from heaven. As creatures of the earth all of us bear the image of Adam, the human comprised of dust. Looking to the future we will all bear the image of Christ, the person from heaven (15:45-49).

This brings us to the high point of Paul's discussion about the resurrection of the body. He is ecstatic about the future life of Christians. He is filled with such hope. Building to a crescendo, he emphasizes twice that all of us, both the living and the dead, "will be changed" (15:51-52). This is the great mystery that God has made known to him. This is the great mystery that God will accomplish. Many in Paul's time and ours as well experience the aging of the body, sometimes afflicted with disease. Energy decreases, muscles weaken, skin wrinkles, mental processes diminish, and memory fades. The good news is that at the resurrection, all will be transformed. We will become a "new creation" (2 Corinthians 5:17). Our resurrected body will be completely animated by the Spirit. It will not perish but will continue forever in the presence of God along with all the saints of God in a state that we can hardly imagine.

Paul then incorporates clothing imagery: the mortal body will put on, like a garment, imperishability and immortality. The resurrected will not be joining the often-capricious immortals of Greek mythology. Rather they will come into the majestic presence of the "immortal, invisible, the only God" (1 Timothy 1:17), whom they "will see face to face" (1 Corinthians 13:12). Up until then, "no eye has seen, nor ear heard, / nor the human heart conceived, / what God has prepared for those who love him" (1 Corinthians 2:9). In the Sermon on the Mount, Jesus calls those who will see God "the pure in heart" (Matthew 5:8). Up until that day, there remains a notable gap between our finite being and the infinite Holy God.

How then should we consider out-of-body or near death experiences (NDEs)? Do they bring a person into contact with the Divine? Since Raymond Moody opened a wider discussion of NDEs in 1975,[42] near death experiences have given rise to a spate of best-selling books and an array of talk-show interviews. In 2012 the Harvard neuroscientist Eben Alexander garnered much attention with his best-selling book *Proof of Heaven: A Neurosurgeon's Journey into the Afterlife.*[43] Having once dismissed NDEs as simply fantasies, he himself reports having an NDE during which he experienced the afterlife and spoke with God. His account is not without controversy, being defended by some and debunked by others. Many who have had NDEs describe entering the "spirit world," seeing loved ones, and encountering ultimate reality. Afterward they speak about changing attitudes and lifestyles, becoming less materialistic and more altruistic.

Paul himself reports an incomprehensible ecstatic experience (not an NDE) that took him up to what he calls the third heaven or paradise. There he "heard things that are not to be told" (2 Corinthians 12:2-4). What Paul and those who have had NDEs experienced can only be known through their own accounts. Each needs to be evaluated carefully. Multiple studies have yielded at least one common effect: the large majority of those who have had an NDE report no longer fearing death.

Death Swallowed Up in Victory

Paul concludes his reflections on the resurrection in chapter 15 by heralding the triumphal defeat of death, drawing upon Isaiah 25:8 and Hosea 13:14: "'Death has been swallowed up in victory.' / 'Where, O death, is your victory? / Where, O death, is your sting?'" (15:54-55). All accolades are to God who achieved the essential victory through Christ Jesus. And this is the foundation for Christians to maintain hope that the same God will be victorious over their death through the resurrection.

In one remarkable passage from Ephesians, Paul shifts from the resurrection as a future event to it already being a present reality. Those who are in Christ have been made "alive together with Christ" (Ephesians 2:5), which is explained in the next verse as being raised up with him: God has "raised us up with him [Christ] and seated us with him [God] in the heavenly places" (verse 6). There is in the Pauline letters an ongoing tension between the "already" and "not yet" of salvation. In Ephesians, he is emphasizing the "already."

Similar to Paul in Ephesians, the Fourth Evangelist also emphasizes the "already." Jesus teaches that those who believe in him already have eternal life (John 3:36). To know that believers enjoy eternal life already in the present is a remarkable thing. The resurrection is still a future event, but authentic life with God is available already now. In the language of Eckhart Tolle this might be: "Enter eternal life now from wherever you are."[44]

The very reason that God sent his Son is "so that everyone who believes in him may not perish but may have eternal life" (John 3:16). Eternal life means much more than the perpetuation of time without end. More profoundly, eternal life refers to an enduring relationship with the one true God: Father, Son, and Holy Spirit. To know God means more than intellectual understanding. It involves a deep relationship of love, trust, and intimacy.

Jesus' teaching that "In my Father's house there are many dwelling places" (John 14:2) implies that eternal life also pertains to our future home in the heavenly realm. As the psalmist reminds us, "Blessed are those who dwell in your house!" (Psalm 84:5, NABRE). I am often struck when patients, particularly the dying, express the desire to go home. Suffering from severe cardiac problems, Marie said to the chaplain, "I am ready to go home." When the chaplain asked if she had someone to take care of her at home, she quickly interrupted, "I mean going to heaven to be with my husband, kids, and other family members." There believers hope to experience reunion with loved ones and with the risen Christ, who has prepared a place for us and who will keep us with him forever.

The final homecoming for believers is beautifully expressed in the ritual for the commendation of a deceased loved one. Calling upon the great cloud of witnesses, the minister prays: "Saints of God, come to her aid! Hasten to meet her, angels of the Lord!" Then addressing the Risen One, the leader continues: "May Christ, who called you, take you to himself; may angels lead you to the bosom of Abraham," a metaphor for the blessed condition in the afterlife (see Luke 16:22-23).

For Reflection:

- In what ways do you experience glimpses of eternal life now? How do you cherish these moments?

- Do you believe that there will be a resurrection of the body? If so, how do you understand this?

Afterword

The themes of life and death course throughout the Bible from generation to generation. Each of us has received the marvelous gift of life, and with each breath we take, our life unfolds. Along our journey we aim to enrich the lives of others through relationship, goodness, and love. Throughout our days we are manifestations of God's image from the very beginning, through the vigor of youth, the flourishing of middle age, to the wisdom gained as we move into our latter years. In the meantime, we live in the present moment with grateful hearts, animated by the Spirit.

Along our journey we remain united to the risen Christ, participating in his death with the hope of someday joining him fully through his resurrection. He is the resurrection and the life. Through our personal losses and the death of loved ones, we have felt the sting of death. And we know that someday we will meet our own death, our final surrender into the outstretched arms of our loving Creator. Until that day may we go forth remembering deep in our hearts that Jesus came so all of us may "have life and have it abundantly" (John 10:10).

May we find the abundance of life by caring for our spirit, attending to our wellbeing. May we, with a merry heart, find time to enjoy a fine glass of wine with family and friends. May we devote our energy day by day, little by little, to the needs of those around us so that they too may enjoy life abundantly. Having poured out our life gener-ously, having run the race faithfully, may we long to hear those welcoming words from the risen Christ, "Well done, my good and faithful servant!" (Matthew 25:21).

Notes

1. *Adversus Haereses* IV, 20, 7.

2. Henri Nouwen, *Our Greatest Gift* (New York: HarperCollins, 1994).

3. Elaine Pagels, *Why Religion?* (New York: HarperCollins, 2018); Julie Yip-Williams, *The Unwinding of the Miracle: A Memoir of Life, Death, and Everything that Comes After* (New York: Random House, 2019).

4. New York: Free Press, 1997.

5. National Library of Medicine, "Greek Medicine," accessed May 12, 2019, https://www.nlm.nih.gov/hmd/greek/greek_oath.html.

6. *The Jewish Study Bible* (Oxford: Oxford University Press, 2004).

7. See William S. Kurz, "Genesis and Abortion: An Exegetical Test of a Biblical Warrant in Ethics," *Theological Studies* 47 (1986) 668-680, pp. 678-679.

8. These are discussed by Richard B. Hays in *The Moral Vision of the New Testament* (New York: HarperCollins, 1996), in chapter 18 on abortion.

9. See William Ross Blackburn's discussion of these references and other biblical texts in "Abortion and the Voice of Scripture," *The Human Life Review* 31.2 (2005): 67-85.

10. Ronald Rolheiser, *The Holy Longing: The Search for a Christian Spirituality* (New York: Doubleday, 1999).

11. Henri Nouwen, *The Return of the Prodigal Son* (London: Darton, Longman & Todd, 1992).

12. "Hans Küng, renowned dissident theologian, considering suicide for Parkinson's," *Life Site News*, October 3, 2013, https://www.lifesitenews.com/news/hans-kung-renowned-dissident-theologian-considering-suicide-for-parkinsons.

13. "Suicide: Redeeming the Memory of a Loved One," July 31, 2017, http://ronrolheiser.com/suicide-redeeming-the-memory-of-a-loved-one/#.W-hfcfZFyM9. See also "Struggling to Understand Suicide," July 28, 2013, https://ronrolheiser.com/struggling-to-understand-suicide/#.XLtNvuhKiM8.

14. Gerhard Lohfink, *Is This All There Is? On Resurrection and Eternal Life* (Collegeville: Liturgical Press, 2017), 115.

15. "Suicide note of renowned Texas priest," *New York Daily News*, accessed April 20, 2019, https://www.nydailynews.com/news/national/suicide-note-texas-priest-accused-molestation-revealed-article-1.2598359.

16. Ethical and Religious Directives for Catholic Health Care Services (ERD), Sixth Edition (2018), p. 20, accessed April 20, 2019, http://www.usccb.org/about/doctrine/ethical-and-religious-directives/upload/ethical-religious-directives-catholic-health-service-sixth-edition-2016-06.pdf.

17. *Ad. Rom.* 4, accessed April 23, 2019, https://www.orderofstignatius.org/files/Letters/Ignatius_to_Romans.pdf.

18. "The Passion of the Holy Martyrs Perpetua and Felicitas," Early Christian Writings, accessed April 23, 2019, http://www.early-christianwritings.com/text/tertullian24.html.

19. Ken Untener, "Prophets of a Future Not Our Own," accessed January 14, 2020, http://www.usccb.org/prayer-and-worship/prayers-and-devotions/prayers/prophets-of-a-future-not-our-own.cfm.

20. Luke Timothy Johnson, "Can We Still Believe in Miracles?," *Commonweal* 146.4 (February 22, 2019), 14-19, p. 17.

21. "The Machinery of Death Is Back on the Docket," *The Atlantic*, September 18, 2018, https://www.theatlantic.com/ideas/archive/2018/09/tinkering-with-the-machinery-of-death/570421/.

22. "New revision of number 2267 of the Catechism of the Catholic Church on the death penalty," accessed April 25, 2019, https://press.vatican.va/content/salastampa/en/bollettino/pubblico/2018/08/02/180802a.html.

23. See Helen Prejean, *Dead Man Walking* (New York: Vintage, 1994); Bryan Stevenson, *Just Mercy* (New York: Penguin Random House, 2014).

24. Henri Nouwen, *Weavings*, November 1992, cited by Michael Leach, et. al. (eds), *The Way of Gratitude* (Maryknoll, NY: Orbis, 2017), 49.

25. On this theme, see Florence M. Gillman, "…Pilate still able to stir up trouble," 25.1 *San Diego Catholic Worker* (2004) 1,4.

26. See the first chapter in Angela Alaino O'Donnell's *Mortal Blessings* (Notre Dame, IN: Ave Marie Press, 2014).

27. Ira Byock, *The Four Things That Matter Most*, 10th Anniversary Edition (New York: Simon and Schuster, 2014).

28. See Carlo Leget, *Art of Living, Art of Dying* (London: Jessica Kingsley, 2017).

29. Christopher P. Vogt, *Practicing Patience, Compassion, and Hope at the End of Life: Mining the Passion of Jesus in Luke for a Christian Model of Dying Well* (Lanham, MD: Rowman & Littlefield, 2004).

30. Allen Verhey, *The Christian Art of Dying: Learning from Jesus* (Grand Rapids: Eerdmans, 2011).

31. "Pope Francis: The resurrection is the most shocking event in human history," *Catholic Herald*, April 22, 2019, https://catholicherald.co.uk/news/2019/04/22/pope-francis-the-resurrection-is-the-most-shocking-event-in-human-history/.

32. "Most Shocking Moments of All Time," The Top Tens, accessed April 29, 2019, https://www.thetoptens.com/most-shocking-moment-of-all-time/.

33. "The 'literal flesh-and-blood' resurrection is the heart of my faith," *America Magazine*, April 23, 2019, https://www.americamagazine.org/faith/2019/04/23/literal-flesh-and-blood-resurrection-heart-my-faith.

34. See "Why the 25% of Christians who deny the resurrection aren't true believers," *Premier Christianity*, April 11, 2017, https://www.

premierchristianity.com/Blog/Why-the-25-of-Christians-who-deny-the-resurrection-aren-t-true-believers.

35. Gerhard Lohfink, *Is This All There Is?*, 90.

36. "Christian Inscriptions in Roman Catacombs," Early Church History, accessed May 2, 2019, https://earlychurchhistory.org/arts/christian-inscriptions-in-roman-catacombs/.

37. "Stephen Hawking: 'There is no heaven; it's a fairy story,'" *The Guardian*, May 15, 2011, https://www.theguardian.com/science/2011/may/15/stephen-hawking-interview-there-is-no-heaven.

38. "Please allow Stephen Hawking to explain time, history, and God," *Quartz*, November 16, 2018, https://qz.com/1464626/please-allow-stephen-hawking-to-explain-time-history-and-god/.

39. For ideas developed in this and the following paragraphs, I am indebted to Gerald O'Collins. See "Our Risen Selves," *America Magazine*, April 9, 2012 Issue, https://www.americamagazine.org/issue/5136/article/our-risen-selves.

40. "What religion does to your brain," *Medical News Today*, July 20, 2018, https://www.medicalnewstoday.com/articles/322539.php.

41. See endnote 40.

42. *Life after Life* (New York: Bantam, 1976).

43. New York: Simon & Schuster, 2012.

44. Eckhart Tolle, *The Power of Now* (Novato, CA: New World Library, 1999).

New City Press

New City Press is one of more than 20 publishing houses sponsored by the Focolare, a movement founded by Chiara Lubich to help bring about the realization of Jesus' prayer: "That all may be one" (John 17:21). In view of that goal, New City Press publishes books and resources that enrich the lives of people and help all to strive toward the unity of the entire human family. We are a member of the Association of Catholic Publishers.

www.newcitypress.com
202 Comforter Blvd.
Hyde Park, New York

Periodicals
Living City Magazine
www.livingcitymagazine.com

Scan to join our mailing list
for discounts and promotions
or go to www.newcitypress.com
and click on "join our email list."